spices

RYLAND
PETERS
& SMALL

LONDON NEW YORK

spices

from the familiar to the exotic—
recipes from around the world

Manisha Gambhir Harkins with photography by Peter Cassidy

First published in USA in 2002
by Ryland Peters & Small, Inc.
519 Broadway, 5th Floor
New York, NY 10012
www.rylandpeters.com

10 9 8 7 6 5 4 3 2 1

Library of Congress Cataloging-in-Publication Data

Harkins, Manisha Gambhir.
Spices : from the familiar to the exotic : recipes
from around the world / Manisha Gambhir Harkins /
photography by Peter Cassidy
        p. cm.
  Includes index.
  ISBN 1-84172-333-9
  1. Cookery (Spices)
  2. Cookery, International. 1. Title.
TX819.A1 H835 2002
641.6'383—dc21   2202021299

Printed and bound in China

Senior Designer Steve Painter
Commissioning Editor Elsa Petersen-Schepelern
Editor Jennifer Herman
Production Patricia Harrington
Art Director Gabriella Le Grazie
Publishing Director Alison Starling

Food Stylist Linda Tubby
Stylist Ròisin Neild
Indexer Hilary Bird

Dedication

To my parents for raising me with such sublime
Indian food, passing down their love of spices and
mom's recipes, and most of all, for their laughter,
unconditional love and support through good times
and bad. And to hubby Billy whose passion for
vindaloo defies hope—thank you for making many a
meal (spices included!) while I typed this book, and
for always being there.

Acknowledgments

Many people provided advice and inspiration:
forgive me if there is any name I forget—I can only
say that my brain is in too many places at once!

Thanks to Elsa and Elizabeth at RPS for having faith
in me, and for Elsa's nurturing through this project.
Thanks to Emi for her Japanese recipe and
knowledge, Makar Gurung at Gurkha Kitchen for his
pumpkin recipe, Clare Ferguson and Linda Collister
for measurement guidance, Marie-Pierre Moine for
info on French spicing, the Lilla Sallskapet
organization in Sweden, and the Indonesian
Embassy. Thanks also to the many tasters including
Morag, John, Lynne, Gordon and wee Daniel,
Deepti, Christiaan (and his lovely parents for Dutch
advice), Jen, Ellen, Berni, Helen, Greg and
Rhiannon in Wales; Amrita and Tibby for numerous
deliciously spiced meals and so very much more,
Gilli for always telling me to go for it and for being
such a great mentor, and all of my aunties in the
States and India for their invaluable culinary
knowledge and love.

Notes

• All spoon measurements are level unless
otherwise stated.
• Ingredients in this book are available from larger
supermarkets, specialty greengrocers, and,
especially, Asian stores and markets. See page
142 for mail order outlets.
• Ovens should be preheated to the specified
temperature. Recipes in this book were tested using
a convection oven. If using a regular oven, cooking
times should be increased according to the
manufacturer's instructions.
• For all recipes requiring dough or batter, liquid
measurements are given as a guide. Always add
liquid gradually to achieve the desired consistency,
rather than adding it all at once. Use your eyes and
your sense of touch to achieve the best results.
Remember that different flours vary in weight. For
example, you will find that masa harina, buckwheat
flour, rice flour, and even wheat flours like superfine
whole-wheat, or fine-textured white bread flour can
weigh less per volume than all-purpose flour. If you
don't use the flour specified in a recipe, the result
may be affected.

Sterilization of preserving jars

• It is essential for health reasons that jars are
sterilized before they are filled with jam or chutney.
• Wash the jars in hot, soapy water and rinse in
boiling water. Put into a large saucepan and cover
with hot water. With the lid on, bring the water to a
boil and continue boiling for 15 minutes. Turn off the
heat, then leave the jars in the hot water until just
before they are to be filled. Invert the jars onto a
clean cloth to dry. Sterilize the lids by boiling for
5 minutes, or according to the manufacturer's
instructions. The jars should be filled and sealed
while they are still hot.
•For useful information on preserving, see website
http://hgic.clemson.edu/factsheets/HGIC3040.htm

contents

spices aren't just fiery . . .

Alluring and scented, mysterious yet familiar, spices heighten the senses and titillate the taste buds. But how does one define a spice? Spices comprise seeds, roots and rhizomes, barks, buds, stigmas, and berries (but not leaves) and, these days, we can buy fresh spice as well as dried. It's a definition that includes all manner of ingredients, from tamarind to fresh ginger, providing us with a large palette from which to work.

Since each spice has its own flavor and aroma, choosing the right one for a regional dish is vital. In addition, certain combinations of spices work beautifully, so if you are new to spice cooking, use mixtures that have been tried and tested, such as an Indian garam masala or an apple pie mix. That said, spices are ripe for experimentation, so enjoy testing for aroma and flavor to get the right balance in a dish.

On page 138 you'll find tips for the purchase, preparation, and use of dried spices and spice mixes, and how to store fresh spices when you can only buy them in large quantities.

In this book, there are recipes using well known blends from around the world, in delicious dishes with a regional stamp—as well as some with just one or two spices. Some recipes may cross cultural boundaries, as similar spicing is used in several areas.

After all, from generation to generation, cooks have always used their intuition to improve or adapt recipes—adding a pinch of chile here or a dash of nutmeg there. Crucially, all these recipes have been created with great joy and relished by willing tasters: I hope you will join them.

the americas

Of all the regions in this book, the Americas are perhaps least known for their use of spices. Yet chiles, vanilla, and allspice were the Americas' spice gifts to the world, while others, such as annatto (achiote) and sassafras bark, have been largely stay-at-homes.

Of non-native spices, cumin was a Spanish introduction and is now perhaps the most common spice after chiles in Central and South America. In the Caribbean, an appealing blend of African, Asian, colonial, and local flavors permeates islanders' cooking. Local allspice appears in many recipes such as Jamaican jerk dishes, while Cajun and Creole cooking have similar influences and share a taste for spicy food.

Nutmeg, cloves, and cinnamon, brought to the Americas by the Spaniards, can be found almost everywhere, although their use is selective. You may find them in Mexican marinades, Argentine sausages, Caribbean sauces, and in North American baking from pies to cookies.

Such spices were all known to the first North American settlers. From Massachusetts to Virginia, early recipes called for spices like coriander, ginger, and mustard. However, just a century later, spice use had declined and plain foods became the norm. Mustard, horseradish, and chiles were exceptions. Later immigrants contributed their own use of spices and today, spices are beginning to make even more of an impact. The exciting urban restaurant culture has given North Americans a taste for foreign flavors and spices, even if they are not necessarily used at home.

the great chile migrations

When Columbus accidentally "discovered" the Americas, it was Spain's quest for Eastern riches and spices, especially the prized black pepper, that allowed the eager Genoese explorer to embark on his adventures. Ferdinand and Isabella of Spain were keen to outwit Portugal by finding a new sea route to the spice riches of India and the East Indies. Looking for a western sea route that would lead him to Asia, Columbus found instead a region that had no connection to the East Indies or the elusive black peppercorn. Yet he mistakenly referred to the new lands as the Indies, the indigenous peoples as Indians, and the fiery new spice/fruit he found, as pepper (*pimiento* in Spanish), while probably knowing full well he would have to make up for his failure to find the real thing. Today we call this incendiary spice the chile or chile pepper, and its globetrotting tale begins in the Americas.

After landing on the West Indian island of Hispaniola in 1492, Columbus wrote to his royal patrons about the many new foods he encountered. He wrote of the chile or *aji*, as it was and still is known regionally, "There is much *aji*, which is their pepper and is worth more than our pepper; no one eats without it because it is very healthy."

When Cortés arrived in Mexico in 1519, he observed the Aztecs eating chiles of all shapes, colors, and sizes (probably around 30 varieties were known there at that time, though chiles had been eaten from around 7500 BC). Similarly, when Pizarro arrived in the land of the Inca, he found the Peruvians eating chiles with gustatory zeal. They were used in soups and stews, along with the vital crops of potatoes and corn, which would later change the world's eating habits. Perhaps the most popular tale about the conquistadors' encounters with the chile is that of the chocolate drink so revered in the court of Montezuma, made with chiles and vanilla, which the Spaniards altered into the hot chocolate we all love today—a perfect example of fusion food!

The Columbian Exchange Like allspice from the Caribbean and vanilla from Central America, chiles became part of the Columbian Exchange (the phenomenon of foods, people, and all manner of goods that were exchanged between New and Old Worlds). Seafaring Iberian merchants soon spread the heat around the globe, taking it to Spanish and Portuguese colonies in Asia and Africa. Most notably, the chile swept India and Southeast Asia.

India and Southeast Asia Both areas were already primed to appreciate the advantages of the chile. They were already devoted to the fiery heat of black pepper and ginger, so the new chile was another spice very much to their taste.

Vasco da Gama had landed at Calicut (Kerala) in 1498, and most sources agree that chiles reached India on Portuguese merchant ships arriving in Goa from 1510. By 1542, three types of capsicums or chiles had been domesticated in India and, apparently, exported to other Asian countries. An Indian observer in the early 16th century described them as the "saviour of the poor, enhancer of good food."

Chiles probably captivated South India first—where the heat of the local black pepper was familiar—before conquering the rest of the subcontinent. Today, India remains the world's largest producer of chiles.

While Spain devoted itself to the gold of the New World, it left the spice trade in the hands of the Portuguese. It was they who supposedly transported the chile from Goa to the Spice Islands of Indonesia and China; the Philippines received it from Spanish-administered Mexico; and possibly from the Philippines the pods moved on to Thailand where

they still reign supreme. It is also highly likely that the Portuguese and Spaniards weren't the only ones to spread the chile. Local merchants used age-old routes to carry chiles as well as other trade goods to neighboring lands.

Moving East In China, Szechuan, which was accustomed to its local fagara "pepper," assimilated the chile into a regional cuisine that became famous for its hot, spicy flavors. Korea fell under the spell of chiles, thanks to Portuguese priests accompanying Japanese troops during the Seven Year War (1592–1599). Japan, in turn, may have acquired the chile via China, as the generic Japanese name of *togarashi* actually means "Chinese mustard." In Asia today, Korea competes with India and Southeast Asia in its claim to be the greatest consumer of chiles, while the Japanese use the dried chile with discretion—mostly in dishes incorporating foreign flavors.

Africa and the Middle East On the Arabian Peninsula, the greatest consumption of chiles has to be in Yemen. With its ancient ties to India, it is no surprise that Yemen grew fond of the chile. Just a hop and a skip across the Red Sea to the Horn of

Africa, most of East Africa, from Ethiopia to Mozambique, were long used to Indian peppercorns as well as their own grains of paradise or melegueta pepper (the name often confused with the malagueta chile of Brazil). Hence when American chiles arrived, they were warmly welcomed and now have "peppered" their cuisines for centuries.

In fact, Africa was assailed from all sides by the blandishments of the chile. The powerful Turkish Ottoman Empire now controlled Constantinople (Istanbul), always one of the great hubs of the spice trade. It was they who took the chile into North Africa and, in Tunisia, this early exposure to chiles resulted in fiery harissa paste—now eaten across the Mahgreb.

West Africa received chiles from those intrepid traders, the Portuguese, who also introduced them to Mozambique in East Africa on their way to the Indies. In South Africa, chiles were brought by Malay slaves to Cape Province as well as by Indian immigrants to Natal. From West Africa to the Cape, from Tunisia to the countries of East Africa, chiles are a passion. Whichever way the spice arrived, it certainly endeared itself to the local population.

Europe As in North Africa, the Ottomans also took the chile into Eastern Europe. Hungarians began producing paprika, while the Ottomans headed further east to Central Asia and Russia with chiles in hand. Besides Spain and Portugal, other people of the Mediterranean also acquired a taste for chiles—witness Provençal sauce rouille served with bouillabaisse, and the sauces of central and southern Italy, especially Sicily, such as arrabbiata and puttanesca.

Despite these European uses of the chile, it is generally in tropical climes that people cling to its fiery heat. Naturally, in places where the pods grew well and where locals were already used to spicy foods, chiles fared best. In fact, Britain may be the exception to the rule, with chutneys and hot Anglo curries—really more British than Indian—that inspire much bravado.

Above, from left: Chile farm producing the raw materials for the famous Tabasco sauce, produced since the mid-1800s by the McIlhennys on Avery Island, Louisiana • The variety used to produce Tabasco is thought to be pequin • Chile stall in Libertat Market, Guadalajara, Jalisco, Mexico, selling the favorite native spice of the Americas.

sweet potato and banana
spiced fritters

A Caribbean idea with its African roots in evidence. Sweet potatoes are great fritter vegetables, melting in your mouth with creamy sweetness. If you can find true plantains (platanos) at a store selling exotic fruit and vegetables, snap them up—they, too, are perfect fritter material. Otherwise, underripe bananas will be convenient substitutes for plantains. Nutmeg (and its outer cover of mace) was originally to be found only in the Spice Islands of Indonesia, but is now one of the major crops of Grenada in the Caribbean.

2 large sweet potatoes
2 plantains or underripe bananas
oil, for deep-frying

Frothy batter

2 cups all-purpose flour
1/2 teaspoon freshly grated nutmeg
2 teaspoons ground cinnamon
about 1 3/4 cups sparkling water

To serve

brown sugar or confectioners' sugar
sweet salsa or chutney

Serves 6–8 (makes about 38)

See note on dough and batter, page 4.

To make the batter, put the flour, nutmeg, and cinnamon into a large bowl and stir well. Make a well in the center and gradually beat in enough sparkling water to make a smooth batter, thick enough to coat the back of a spoon. Cover with a dish towel and set aside for 20 minutes.

Cut the sweet potatoes into 1/2-inch slices, then cut in half (you should have about 28 half-moon pieces). Cut the plantains or bananas into 1-inch slices (about 10) because they will cook much faster.

Fill a deep saucepan one-third full of oil and heat to 375°F or until a cube of bread browns in 30 seconds. Working in batches and using tongs, dip a piece of plantain or banana into the batter, coat well, then slide it into the hot oil—do not overcrowd the pan. Fry until golden brown all over. Remove with a slotted spoon, drain in a colander lined with paper towels, then transfer to a serving plate and keep them warm while you cook the sweet potatoes, again in batches.

Sprinkle with sugar and serve hot. These fritters are great on their own, but you can also serve them with sweet salsa or chutney.

cajun-spiced chowder
with corn and bacon

4 ears of corn or 2 cups fresh or frozen kernels

2 tablespoons unsalted butter

1 onion, finely chopped

1 small celery stalk, finely chopped

4–5 slices bacon, chopped

1½ teaspoons Cajun Spice Blend (American Spice Mixes, page 32)

5 cups vegetable stock

1 cup light cream

To serve

2 tablespoons freshly chopped oregano

an extra pinch of Cajun Spice Blend

crusty bread

green salad

Serves 4

Chowders are creamy, chunky soups, the most famous of which is New England clam chowder. Corn chowders are popular too—a real taste of America. In this version, I've looked to the Deep South for inspiration: the result is Louisiana soul food with just the right amount of Acadian (Cajun country) spice.

Here in the States, commercial spice blends can be a long way from their original form. Cajun spice blends are an example—some brands are not bad, while others add far too much cayenne, and sometimes totally unnecessary MSG. It is very easy to make your own blend—remembering that the three peppers (white, black, and cayenne) are essential, when properly balanced, to the Cajun way of spicing. Celery salt is also part of the blend, so extra salt is not necessary.

If using fresh ears of corn, remove the husks and silks and cut the stalk end flat. Put the flat end on a board and cut off the kernels from top to bottom. Discard the cobs.

Melt the butter in a large saucepan, add the onion, and sauté for 5 minutes. Add the celery and sauté for a further 3 minutes until well softened. Add the bacon and cook for 1–2 minutes. Add the corn and Cajun spice blend and mix well.

Add the vegetable stock and bring to a boil. Reduce the heat and simmer for about 35 minutes. Add the cream and simmer until thickened. You can serve the soup immediately or, to thicken it further, put a ladle of the chowder (without any of the bacon) into a blender and purée until smooth. Pour the blended chowder back into the saucepan and mix well.

To serve, ladle into bowls and top with a little oregano and a very light dusting of Cajun spice blend. Serve hot with crusty bread and a green salad.

butternut squash soup
with allspice and pine nuts

1 medium butternut squash, halved lengthwise and seeded

2 tablespoons unsalted butter

1 large leek, trimmed and chopped

1 bay leaf

a few black peppercorns, crushed

4–5 allspice berries, crushed

2¾ cups vegetable stock

¾ cup pine nuts, toasted in a dry skillet

crusty bread, to serve

a nonstick baking tray

Serves 4

Squashes and allspice are native to the Americas and pine nuts have been gathered in the deserts of the Southwest for at least a thousand years. This is a quintessentially American soup, popular in both north and south. Growing up in the Northeast, I've tasted squash soups throughout the region, from Connecticut to Massachusetts, and what better comfort on a crisp fall day in New England? The key to this soup is the light spicing and the roasting of the butternut squash to bring out the best of its sweet flavor.

Put the butternut squash halves flesh side down onto the baking tray. Roast in a preheated oven at 375°F for 45 minutes or until tender. Remove from the oven and, using a spoon, scoop the flesh out of the skins into a bowl. Discard the skins.

Put the butter into a large saucepan and melt over medium to low heat. Add the leek, bay leaf, peppercorns, and allspice and sauté until the leek begins to soften. Add the butternut squash, stock, and 1 quart water. Bring to a boil, reduce the heat, and simmer for about 10 minutes, or until the leeks are very soft.

Remove the bay leaf and transfer the soup to a blender. Add the pine nuts and blend until smooth, working in batches if necessary. Return the soup to the saucepan and reheat. Serve hot with crusty bread.

burritos with black beans and avocado salsa

3 garlic cloves

1 cup dried black beans, soaked overnight and drained

2 chipotle chiles

2 tablespoons corn or olive oil

1½ teaspoons cumin seeds

2 sprigs of epazote or winter savory (optional)

1 onion, finely chopped

2–4 scallions, chopped

sea salt and freshly ground black pepper

Avocado and red onion salsa

1 Hass avocado

freshly squeezed juice of 1 lime

1 large red onion, chopped

10 cherry tomatoes, quartered

½ teaspoon sugar

¼ cup chopped fresh cilantro

Corn tortillas*

2 cups masa harina

a pinch of salt

1 tablespoon olive oil

To serve

a handful of cilantro, chopped

a handful of shredded lettuce

crème fraîche or plain yogurt

*flour tortillas (if not making recipe above)

**Serves 6 as an appetizer
or 3 as an entrée**

See note on dough and batter, page 4.

We have Mexico to thank for the introduction of chiles to the rest of the world—innumerable varieties of chiles, from the fresh green fiery serrano to the fruity mahogany-colored dried ancho. This recipe calls for smoky chipotle chile, as well as cumin, in a cuisine that features herbs like epazote and cilantro more than spices. If you don't like masa harina, you might prefer to buy flour tortillas and follow the package instructions.

Put 2 of the garlic cloves and the beans into a saucepan, add enough water to cover the beans by 1 inch, bring to a boil, reduce the heat, cover, and cook for 1½–2 hours or until the beans are very tender (cooking time depends on the age of the beans). Drain the beans, reserving the cooking liquid.

Crush the remaining garlic and chop one of the chiles. Heat the oil in a large saucepan and add the chiles, cumin, and epazote, if using. Sauté for 20 seconds, then add the onion. Sauté for about 5 minutes, then add the crushed garlic. Cook for a further 3–4 minutes or until the onion is soft. Add the drained beans, together with a little of their cooking liquid to keep them moist. Continue to cook, stirring frequently. Add the salt and pepper and mash well, adding enough liquid to make a chunky paste. Cover.

To make the salsa, scoop out the avocado flesh and cut into smallish chunks. Put it into a bowl with the lime juice, tossing well so the avocado doesn't discolor. Add the red onion, cherry tomatoes, and avocado, then stir in the sugar and cilantro. Mix well, cover, and set aside.

To make the tortillas, put the masa harina, salt, and oil into a mixing bowl with a lid. Gradually stir in about 1 cup water—enough to bind the mixture together to form a dough. Knead briefly, then shape into a ball, cover, and set aside for several minutes.

Knead the dough again and divide into 6 balls, keeping them covered with a lid or plate over the bowl while working. Flatten one and roll out between 2 sheets of plastic wrap. Heat a nonstick skillet until hot. Put the tortilla into the pan and cook for 45 seconds, until the edges begin to dry out. Turn it over and cook for about 30 seconds more. Turn it over one more time and cook for 10 seconds. Remove and keep the tortilla warm in a dish towel or foil while you cook the remainder.

Gently reheat the beans, add the scallions and cilantro, and stir gently. Put a small portion of beans onto each tortilla and carefully roll into a burrito. Put a little salsa onto each plate. Let guests help themselves to the lettuce and crème fraîche or yogurt.

jerk chicken

There are as many jerk chicken recipes in Jamaica as there are cooks, but all include the fiery Scotch bonnet chile or the closely related habanero, plus a good dose of native allspice. Jerk seasoning also includes nutmeg, a native of the Spice Islands of Indonesia (page 118), grown in the West Indies since the 19th century. Today, jerk huts along the beaches are a magnet for tourists. Traditionally grilled over wood, jerk chicken—or pork—can easily be cooked on any outdoor grill or in the oven.

4 chicken legs (thigh and drumstick)

1 recipe Jerk Seasoning Paste*
(American Spice Mixes, page 33)

To serve

lemon or lime wedges

buttered rolls

Serves 4

Cut slashes in the chicken legs and spread with half the jerk seasoning paste. Rub the paste all over and into the slashes, cover, and marinate in the refrigerator for at least 2 hours or overnight.

Put the chicken legs skin side down into a roasting pan. Roast in a preheated oven at 400°F for 40–45 minutes or until crisp and cooked through, turning halfway through the cooking time and coating with the remaining marinade.

Alternatively, preheat a charcoal grill until very hot. Cook the chicken over high heat to begin with, then adjust the rack further away from the fire as soon as the surfaces of the chicken have begun to brown. Cook for 15–20 minutes or until done, turning frequently and basting with the remaining marinade. You must cook poultry thoroughly so there is no pink inside: if you have an instant-read thermometer, it should read 165°F when inserted into the thickest part of the thigh.

Serve hot with lemon or lime wedges and soft buttered rolls.

Note Jerk seasoning includes native Caribbean allspice and nutmeg brought from the Spice Islands. Allspice is a dried red berry, said to be redolent of nutmeg, cinnamon, and cloves, hence "all-spice." It has a special fragrance, and is popular in the cooking of some European countries, such as Britain and Denmark, with former colonies in the West Indies. Nutmeg was smuggled out of the Spice Islands, breaking the Dutch stranglehold on its trade, and has been grown in the Caribbean since the 19th century.

argentine barbecued chimichurri beef

4 sirloin or T-bone steaks

sea salt and freshly ground black pepper

olive oil, for brushing

Chimichurri parsley base

3 cups fresh flat-leaf parsley, trimmed of tough stalks and coarsely chopped

2 large garlic cloves, quartered

1/2 teaspoon sweet pimentón (Spanish oak-smoked paprika)

1/4 teaspoon freshly grated nutmeg

a pinch of ground cinnamon

a pinch of chili powder or hot red pepper flakes

2 tablespoons freshly squeezed lemon juice

1/2 cup extra virgin olive oil or corn oil

sea salt, to taste

Dressing

1/2 small onion, finely chopped

3/4 teaspoon superfine sugar

1 teaspoon freshly squeezed lemon juice

1 red bell pepper, finely chopped (about 1/3 cup)

1/4 teaspoon freshly grated nutmeg

2 tablespoons extra virgin olive oil or corn oil

Serves 4

Argentine beef is legendary, thanks to the seemingly endless grazing land of the pampas and the country's own brand of cowboys, the gauchos. These oft-romanticized characters have left a strong imprint on local food traditions. Beef is often cooked on a *parrilla*—a large barbecue grill—and served on its own or with condiments like chimichurri. Argentines have many versions of this parsley-based sauce/relish; some include nutmeg, cinnamon, or cumin, while others are without spice. Like most South Americans, however, they take pride in local chiles. Chimichurri contains a native chile, aji molido, which is unique in its mellow, sweet, smoky heat. Since it is rare in other parts of the world, I have substituted Spanish sweet pimentón (paprika), plus hot red pepper flakes or chili powder. Of course, if you have access to aji molido, then go for the real thing! Serve the steaks with accompaniments such as grilled vegetables and baked potatoes, which can be cooked in the coals.

To make the chimichurri parsley base, put all the ingredients into a blender and work to a smooth sauce. Alternatively use a mortar and pestle.

Put the chopped onion into a bowl, add the sugar and lemon juice, and stir well. Cover and set aside for at least 30 minutes. Add the pimentón (paprika), nutmeg, oil, and 3–4 tablespoons of the chimichurri base. Mix well and set aside. (Save any remaining chimichurri base for use as a pesto-type topping, or pour into ice cube trays, freeze, and use for flavoring stocks, soups, and stews.)

To prepare the beef, preheat a charcoal grill until very hot (you can add oak or hickory chips if available) and brush the steaks with a little oil. Cook over high heat to begin with, then adjust the rack further away from the fire as soon as the surfaces of the steaks have begun to sear. Cook to your liking, turning once during cooking. Alternatively, cook under a preheated broiler or on a stove-top grill pan. Sprinkle with salt and pepper and serve hot with the chimichurri.

Variation Finely chop 1 poblano or other mild green chile and mix with the chimichurri.

classic apple pie

America is a nation of pie lovers—peach, cherry, blueberry, pecan, pumpkin, and so forth—and most familiar of all is the good ol' apple pie. It is so entrenched in our psyche, that the phrase "apple pie" has come to mean "wholesome" and "all-American." Apples and spices are meant for each other: cloves and cinnamon elevate this pie to another level.

5 cooking apples, such as Rome or Empire

freshly squeezed juice of 1 lemon

1 cup sugar, plus extra to serve

2 teaspoons ground cinnamon

4 whole cloves

milk, for brushing

vanilla ice cream or light cream, to serve

Dough

2¼ cups all-purpose flour, sifted, plus extra for dusting

a pinch of salt

1½ sticks unsalted butter, chilled and cut into pieces

a metal pie plate, 9 inches diameter*

Serves 4–6

See note on dough and batter, page 4*

*Pie plates vary in performance. Many people use glass or ceramic pie plates, but the best heat conductor is the old fashioned metal plate (for even cooking). Stainless steel pie plates and tart pans also perform well.

To make the dough, put the flour and salt into a large bowl. Working lightly, rub in the butter with your fingertips until the mixture resembles bread crumbs. Alternatively, use a food processor. Add just enough cold water (about 3–4 tablespoons) to bring the dough together. Gently form into a ball, wrap in plastic, and refrigerate for 20 minutes.

Remove the dough from the refrigerator and divide into 2 balls, one slightly larger than the other. Put the larger piece of dough onto a lightly floured surface and, using a rolling pin, gently flatten it out into a round. Roll out and use to line the pie plate, leaving about 1 inch overhang. Prick the base all over with a fork.

Peel, core, and slice the apples into a bowl, tossing them in lemon juice as you work to stop them discoloring. Mix the sugar and cinnamon in a bowl, then put half the apples into the pie plate and sprinkle half the sugar and cinnamon mixture over the top. Arrange the remaining apples on top and sprinkle with the remaining sugar and cinnamon. Dot the cloves on top.

Roll out the remaining dough and use to cover the pie. Crimp the edges together with your fingers to seal and trim off any excess. Pierce the lid and brush with a little milk.

Bake in a preheated oven at 425ºF for 15 minutes, then lower the heat to 350ºF and bake for a further 25–30 minutes, or until the pastry is golden brown and the apples are well cooked. Sprinkle with extra sugar and serve hot with vanilla ice cream or light cream.

mexican chocolate
with vanilla cream

4 oz. bittersweet chocolate, broken into pieces

6 cups whole milk

¼ cup sugar

2 teaspoons ground cinnamon

cinnamon sticks, to serve (optional)

Vanilla whipped cream

1 cup heavy cream

1 vanilla bean*

Serves 6

Don't throw away the vanilla bean after use. Put it into a storage container and cover with sugar to make vanilla sugar.

In Mexico, hot chocolate has always been known simply as "chocolate," and it was here of course that the world's love affair with the addictively good substance began. The Aztecs, like the Olmecs before them, used the cacao bean only for the drink, making it with water, sometimes adding native vanilla, and even chiles. The conquistadors altered the recipe to include sugar, cinnamon (showing the Moorish influence in Spain), and supposedly anise and pepper, the latter presumably to replace the hotter chile. Today Mexican chocolate is a hybrid, closer to the hot cocoa we all know and love. Mexicans use real chocolate pieces made with sugar, cinnamon, and almonds. I follow their tradition by using top quality chocolate—at least 70 percent cocoa solids and organic/fairtrade on principle (see note)—and perfuming the resulting elixir with cinnamon.

To make the vanilla whipped cream, put the cream into a bowl and beat with an electric beater until light and fluffy, with soft peaks. Slit the vanilla bean lengthwise and carefully scrape out all the seeds. Gently fold them into the cream.

To make the hot chocolate, put the chocolate into a heatproof bowl set over a saucepan of gently simmering water and melt—don't let the bowl touch the water or the chocolate will be spoiled. Pour the milk into a large saucepan and stir in the sugar and cinnamon. Heat until gently simmering—do not boil. Beat a ladle of the milk into the melted chocolate, then pour the mixture into the saucepan, beating until smooth. Ladle into 6 mugs. Top each with a generous spoonful of vanilla whipped cream and serve hot with a cinnamon stick stirrer, if using.

Note Buy organic and fairtrade chocolate whenever you can. Organic brands are produced without lindane, a harmful hormone-disrupting pesticide that may soon be banned in Europe. The fairtrade mark makes a stand against the chocolate slave trade going on in the Ivory Coast and nearby. If you can, question the origins of the chocolate you are buying, make a stand, and make a difference.

bloody mary

1 cup vodka

2 cups tomato juice

3½–4 tablespoons lemon juice

½ teaspoon Tabasco, or to taste

1 teaspoon Worcestershire sauce, or to taste

a pinch of freshly ground white pepper

To serve

ice cubes

4 celery stalks

few celery leaves, finely chopped (optional)

Serves 4

Although there are chile sauces the world over, none is as instantly recognizable as Tabasco, from Avery Island in Louisiana, where the McIlhenny family have been producing the fiery mixture since 1868. A mixture of "tabasco" (supposedly pequín) chiles, vinegar, and salt, the sauce is aged in oak barrels. Just as the story of chiles is intertwined with the Americas as a whole, Tabasco is inextricably linked with the US, used to spice everything from oysters to the ever-popular Bloody Mary.

Put all the ingredients into a blender, blend, then pour into 4 glasses half-filled with ice cubes. Alternatively, put the ingredients into a cocktail shaker, add ice, shake, and strain into glasses of fresh ice cubes. Add a celery stalk and a few chopped celery leaves, if using, to each glass, then serve.

mulled apple cider

1 quart unsweetened apple juice

1 cinnamon stick

3 black peppercorns

8 whole cloves

12 allspice berries

Serves 4

In New England, mulled apple cider is a favorite fall drink. From Connecticut up to Vermont, you'll encounter this hot spiced drink, often served with sugar doughnuts. Look for apple cider mills dotting the region.

Put the apple juice into a saucepan and add the cinnamon, peppercorns, cloves, and allspice. Warm gently for 10 minutes and let stand for at least 15 minutes, or longer if you have the time. (The longer it is left to stand, the stronger the infusion.) Just before serving, heat to almost boiling, then simmer gently for 1 minute. Strain into 4 heatproof glasses or mugs and serve hot with doughnuts or pastries.

chilito

¼ teaspoon pasilla chile flakes, with seeds

1 dried chipotle chile, seeded and chopped

6 thick slices jalapeño in brine
or 1 large fresh jalapeño, seeded

about 5 large cabbage leaves, trimmed of
tough stalks

1 small onion

1 tablespoon chopped fresh oregano
or marjoram

3 tablespoons white wine vinegar*

3 tablespoons rice vinegar*

⅓ cup pineapple juice

sea salt, to taste

Serves 6 as a relish

*Traditionally, chilitos are often made in
Mexico with mild tropical fruit vinegars like
pineapple vinegar. If you have such vinegars
available, try them out.*

Chilito is an aptly named crunchy relish from Mexico made with two or three chile varieties. It reveals the nuances of various chiles, and brings their individual flavors, not just their heat, to the fore. I've used licorice-like pasilla chile flakes, smoky chipotle chiles, and jalapeño slices. Feel free to use just two varieties—the jalapeño and one other.

Soak the dried pasilla and chipotle chiles in 2 teaspoons warm water for about 15 minutes, then drain. Finely chop the jalapeños. Set aside.

Finely shred the cabbage in a food processor and transfer to a bowl. Repeat with the onion and add to the bowl. Add the oregano, 3 kinds of chiles, and salt and toss well.

Mix the vinegars and juice in a small bowl and add to the bowl. Mix very well (the liquid is just enough to coat the vegetables—it is not meant to submerge them). Set aside for 1–2 hours to develop the flavors. Serve a little chilito on the side with Mexican entrée dishes, burritos (page 19), or corn chips, together with other condiments.

salsa roja

12 dried New Mexico chiles

½ cup safflower oil

3 garlic cloves, halved

1 tablespoon chopped fresh oregano

6 large, ripe tomatoes, peeled and seeded

sea salt and freshly ground black pepper

corn chips, to serve

Makes about 2 cups

Mexican restaurants and homes everywhere keep this sauce or condiment on the table or beside the stove. Add it to anything you think needs a bit of livening up, or serve with corn chips and margaritas or Bloody Mary (page 29). New Mexico chiles have a smoky, earthy flavor, but they aren't overly hot: use other, hotter dried chiles if you prefer—try chipotle, ancho, pasilla, or cascabel.

Break the chiles in half and shake out the seeds. Heat the oil in a skillet, add the chiles and sauté until they turn bright red. Remove with a slotted spoon and put into a bowl. Cover with water and let soak for about 30 minutes.

Add the garlic to the pan and sauté until golden. Transfer to a food processor, add the drained chiles, and chop coarsely. Add the oregano and tomatoes and chop again. Add salt and pepper to taste and serve with corn chips.

american spice mixes

From apple pie spice to Jamaican jerk seasoning, from Mexican salsas to barbecue sauce—although based on traditional blends, these mixes are most widely known in their commercial forms. Many of their ingredients are in fact native to the Americas—where would spice lovers be without chiles, cayenne, Tabasco, vanilla, or allspice. Some of these mixes are used in the recipes in this book: others are included for you to try in other dishes.

Cajun Spice Blend

A blend based on the three peppers—black, white, and native cayenne. It flavors everything from blackened fish to hearty gumbo and jambalaya, and can also be used as a barbecue rub for chicken and meat.

¼ teaspoon black peppercorns

¼ teaspoon white peppercorns

½ teaspoon cumin seeds

½ teaspoon coriander seeds

½ teaspoon cayenne pepper

½ teaspoon paprika

½ teaspoon celery salt

Crush the whole spices with a mortar and pestle until coarsely ground. Add the cayenne, paprika, and celery salt and mix well.

Mexican Recado

A marinade for grilled meat, especially beef. It can be confusing because there are recado marinades and recado-based sauces. Recado marinade is far too pungent to be served raw, and is usually grilled on the meat.

1 small piece of cinnamon or cassia bark

1 teaspoon cumin seeds

½ teaspoon black peppercorns

2 allspice berries

½–1 very hot chile, such as habanero or malagueta, seeded and chopped

a small sprig of oregano

4–5 garlic cloves, chopped

1 small red onion, coarsely chopped

¼ cup extra virgin olive oil

¼ cup white wine vinegar or a combination of fresh lime and lemon juice

a pinch of salt

Put the cinnamon or cassia, cumin, peppercorns, and allspice into a dry skillet and toast until aromatic. Transfer to a blender, add the remaining ingredients, and blend until smooth. Use 1–2 tablespoons as a marinade and also use to baste the meat.

Crab or Fish Boil Spices

Packs of spice mixes like this are sold in supermarkets, for you to add to the water in which crab, fish, or shrimp are cooked. Try my recipe using fresh spices, or add extras to your own taste.

1 teaspoon caraway seeds

1 teaspoon coriander seeds

1 teaspoon whole cloves

1 teaspoon allspice berries

1 teaspoon black peppercorns

1 teaspoon mustard seeds

1 bay leaf

Put all the spices into a cheesecloth bag or meshed spice ball—the bag or ball can be removed before serving.

Jerk Seasoning Paste

This typical Jamaican seasoning is spread over meat (especially pork), poultry, or fish before it is grilled or baked. It includes the native spices—allspice and chiles.

3–4 habanero chiles, seeded

1 teaspoon chopped fresh thyme

3 garlic cloves, coarsely chopped

1 bay leaf

1 teaspoon allspice berries (about 20)

¼ teaspoon freshly grated nutmeg

3 scallions, chopped

2 plum tomatoes, peeled (fresh or canned)

freshly squeezed juice of ½ lime

⅓ cup peanut oil

½ teaspoon salt

Using a blender or mortar and pestle, grind the ingredients to a smooth paste. Use immediately or store in the refrigerator for up the 2 days.

Poudre de Colombo

A curry powder from Guadeloupe and Martinique. The original was brought over by Indian migrants, many from East India, to make a curry known as Colombo. The formula has changed and now has a definite Caribbean stamp.

¼ teaspoon ground turmeric

4 dried chiles or 2 fresh chiles

1½ teaspoons coriander seeds

1½ teaspoons brown mustard seeds

4 black peppercorns

1 teaspoon long-grain rice, toasted in a dry skillet until aromatic

3–4 garlic cloves

Grind everything but the garlic to a fine powder. Mash in the garlic and either use immediately or within a day.

BARBECUE SPICES
Marinades, Rubs, and Glazes

You can't beat a barbecue for flavor, fun, and smoky aromas filling the backyard. The recipes here are typical, however many of the spice blends in other chapters of this book can also be used as rubs—they just require a little experimentation. Use Cajun Spice Blend (opposite) in this way.

Basic Herb and Spice Rub

Good for beef and lamb.

¼ teaspoon celery salt

½ teaspoon chili powder or cayenne pepper

leaves from a small sprig of marjoram (or a few large oregano leaves)

leaves from a 2-inch sprig of rosemary

⅛ teaspoon caraway seeds

¼ teaspoon paprika

2 bay leaves

5 black peppercorns

½ teaspoon mustard seeds

Using a small blender or mortar and pestle, grind all the ingredients to a powder. Use as soon as possible, while the herbs are fresh. Alternatively, if keeping for longer, use dried herbs, but halve the quantity.

Mustard Molasses Glaze

A sweet, sharp glaze or basting sauce for grilled steak or spareribs. I like to use light brown rather than dark, to avoid increasing the molasses flavor, which can become rather bitter.

2 tablespoons Dijon mustard

2 tablespoons molasses

1 tablespoon balsamic vinegar

1 tablespoon light brown sugar

Put all the ingredients into a small saucepan and heat, stirring, for about 1 minute or until slightly syrupy.

Mustard, Honey, and Cider Vinegar Glaze

A great sticky glaze for pork.

3 tablespoons mild mustard

3 tablespoons honey

1 tablespoon cider vinegar

Put all the ingredients into a small saucepan and heat, stirring, for 2–3 minutes until thick and syrupy.

Molasses Mustard Glaze for Beef

2 tablespoon Dijon mustard

1 tablespoon soft brown sugar

1 tablespoon balsamic vinegar

Put all the ingredients into a saucepan and heat slowly, stirring. Bring to a boil and simmer gently for 1 minute, until slightly thickened and syrupy.

europe

Europe, it seems, has always had a passion for spices. Their use in Europe dates back at least as far as Ancient Greece and Rome, when spices were held in the highest esteem. When Alexander the Great conquered the Phoenicians' great city of Tyre, in what is now Lebanon, he also took control of the early spice routes. Ever since, spices have been in great demand in Europe, with battles waged, new routes charted, and mighty ships racing to establish a monopoly over this profitable trade. After the Greeks came the Romans, with their passion for pepper, the Venetians with their passion for money, and then the Portuguese, Spaniards, Dutch, and English, all with their avid hunger first for spices, then for colonies.

It was when those adventurers returned home that the true complexity of foreign spices was included in the kitchens and later restaurant cultures of Europe. Think of Britain in particular, where returning officers of the East India Company and the Raj in India and Malaya brought home the curry powder, chutney, and other approximations of the brilliant flavors they had found on the other side of the world.

Eventually, Europe became home to more than just the spices—they were soon joined by the food and the people too. As well as Britain with its curry and chutney, Holland has rijsttafel, France has incorporated the flavors of Vietnam and North Africa, Spain the influences of the Moors and the Americas, and Portugal has half the world eating chiles.

the merchants of venice

Venice's centuries-long hold over Mediterranean and European trade routes is still a marvel, reflected today in the splendor of her Grand Canal. As the Renaissance dawned, Venice had already established herself as the crossroads of the spice trade between Europe and the East, a republic brimming with riches—the envy of the Continent. She had inherited the earlier Greco-Roman spice trade, but soon, along with the rest of medieval Europe, her envious eyes fell upon the rich and radiant Islamic world. The East shone like a luminous but distant star, full of lustrous commodities from cloves and cardamom to damask and gems. Spices beckoned even at great expense, and someone had to supply the spice-starved denizens of Europe. Hence, Venice's rise as the great Western ambassador—a sturdy bridge between East and West.

Finding a foothold But how did Venice gain such a foothold in the spice trade at a time when the rest of Europe was mired in the Dark Ages, encircled by barbarians, and closed off by what many called the "Muslim curtain"? There were many reasons for her steady growth as Europe's mighty commercial power, including her island status,

seamanship, prime position on the Adriatic, not to mention monopolistic goals. The city was born of a fractious group of islands, which came together as a federation in the fifth century, when mainlanders fled the barbarian hordes sweeping Italy. The same lagoons that offered refuge were the foundation of what was to become the "Serene Republic" of Venice. Even as early as the eighth century, while things were amiss elsewhere, Venetians were building their famous, slender galleys and beginning to prosper via trade with Mediterranean ports.

At the same time, Venice was caught between the mainland and the Franks on the one hand, and Byzantium and the East on the other. Yet the young Republic proved surprisingly resilient, swaying between forces when necessary, yet always asserting her independence. In the beginning, her allegiance to Byzantium meant Venetian merchants held valuable commercial rights. Later, a Frankish alliance with the Papacy worked against Venetian interests, as the Republic was barred from trading with former mainland allies. However, Venice managed to repel a Frankish invasion in 810, giving Venice freedom to grow of her own accord. And grow she did.

Queen of the Adriatic Venice took advantage of the peace which ensued to expand her trading interests and, as a result, her wealth and power. Pivotally, Rialto (modern-day Venice), which had sheltered Venetians so well, became the capital—and the first harbor of Venice. Boxes of spices, casks of wines, and a plethora of goods were unloaded from the Grand Canal then stored in fondaci (warehouses).

Although the Republic of Venice was ruled by Doges, her nouveau riche merchant class grew more powerful through her commercial clout. The merchants' influence was considerable. They prospered especially after the Fourth Crusade, after which (1204), Venice divided the spoils amongst several eminent families. A number of Venice's large personalities, including one or two of the Doges, may have belonged to old money, but often went on after their education into service on the trading galleys. The Crusades fostered further interest in the spices and luxuries of the East. Venice profited greatly from this renewed demand, and for the fact that it was Europe's buttress against the Turks. The Republic was also in a good position after defeating pirates in the Adriatic, and via its

acquisition of several Greek islands and a portion of Constantinople.

Venice's command of the surrounding seas made her practically invincible. Venetian merchants traveled freely to the ports of Egypt, the Levant, and Constantinople. They traded their own famous woolen cloth, laces, soaps, and glass for the spices, nuts, and fruits of Lebanon, Syria, Aleppo, and Alexandria, precious metals from North Africa, and silk and other goods from Constantinople. Such goods reached the Venetians, via the Arabs, from the South China Sea, Indian Ocean, and Arabian Sea. During her heyday, Venice imported almost 400,000 lb. of spices each year. Not only did she trade within the Mediterranean, she was the great distributor of spices and silks to all of Europe. Her galleys reached France, Flanders, and England.

At around the same time, a remarkable change had taken place in the Orient. The Mongols had swept the Middle East and Asia, wreaking havoc, but also fostering multiculturalism and freedom of religion, to the distaste of Christian Europe. While the sea routes beyond the Mediterranean leading to the actual sources of spices were barred to Venetians, the ancient Silk

Road was reopened for just a century (about 1250–1350), during which Italian merchants could travel overland under Tartar protection across Central Asia through Persia, Afghanistan, China, and India, buying their spices at source. The most famous was Marco Polo, who set off from Venice with his father and uncle in 1271, returning after 24 years, having served under the famous Chinese Mongol Emperor, Kublai Khan. Marco himself was a product of Venice—nephew of a rich merchant who held trading houses in the Crimea and Constantinople. Via his chronicles, *Description of the World*, the peripatetic Venetian opened Europe's eyes to a fascinating world of lapis lazuli, the fabled Xanadu, gems, silks, and spices.

Venice's sea routes, however, soon became her sole source of spices once more. She absorbed her neighbors and even managed to secure treaties with the Turks to ensure the safety of her commercial colonies for a time.

As long as the West relied on the Mediterranean as its prime trade route, Venice could count on her supremacy. She secured her power by any means; through threats of boycott, double taxation, protectionism, and ensuring that all commodities, no matter where

they originated, or their destination, had to come to Venice first. All other merchants had to buy the goods from Venetians. Venice was indisputably Queen, with a veritable monopoly on the spice trade.

Good things don't last forever, as they say. Yet even after great damage to her commercial interests due to the new Portuguese spice route around the Cape, from 1550, Venice saw 30 years of renewed and vigorous Mediterranean commerce. However, after this time, the Republic's decline was inevitable. The spice race was on, and the slender Venetian galleys were no match for the Cape route or the mighty galleons that would soon follow its course. In Europe, the time for Portugal, Spain, England, and Holland had come.

Above, from left: From the end of the Crusades to the discovery of the sea route around the Cape of Good Hope, Venice and her Arab partners held the monopoly of the spice trade • Saffron was introduced to Spain by the Phoenicians, and it is now the major source of this expensive spice • Saffron threads are the stigmas of the saffron crocus. The reason for its cost is that it must be picked by hand early in the morning before the sun comes up and dries the pollen in the flowers.

andalusian chickpea soup
with chorizo, paprika, and saffron

2 tablespoons extra virgin olive oil

1 medium onion, chopped

3 thin celery stalks, chopped, with leaves reserved

1 large carrot, chopped

2 garlic cloves, chopped

8 oz. chorizo sausage, skinned, halved, then cut into ½-inch slices (or use a mixture of chorizo and another Southern European sausage, such as morcilla or Italian sausages)

1 can chickpeas, drained, 14 oz.

7 cups chicken stock

¼ teaspoon hot pimentón (Spanish oak-smoked paprika)*

4 oz. spinach, tough stalks removed and leaves coarsely chopped into large pieces, about 1 cup

¼ teaspoon saffron threads, bruised with a mortar and pestle

Serves 4 as an entrée

This hearty soup is a meal in itself. Chunks of chorizo and perhaps other sausages such as morcilla jostle with chickpeas and spinach in a slightly smoky, fragrant broth. The special flavor comes from two typically Spanish spices, pimentón (Spanish oak-smoked paprika, made from a variety of bell pepper) and its home-grown luxury spice, saffron. Although saffron is grown in many parts of the world, from Kashmir to Turkey, it is said that the best comes from La Mancha in Central Spain.

Heat the oil in a large saucepan and add the onion, celery, and carrot. Gently sauté the vegetables until they begin to soften. Add the garlic, chorizo, chickpeas, stock, and paprika. Bring to a boil, reduce the heat, and simmer for about 10 minutes. Add the spinach and celery leaves and simmer for a further 15 minutes.

Add the saffron and clean out the mortar using a little of the stock. (I don't like to waste even the tiniest speck of expensive saffron!) Add to the saucepan and simmer for another 5 minutes. Serve hot in large, wide bowls as an entrée. Add shavings of cheese, if using. This soup is very filling, but some good crusty bread and perhaps some extra cheese make delightful partners.

chicken quatre épices

2 tablespoons unsalted butter

2 tablespoons extra virgin olive oil

3 lb. chicken, cut into 8 pieces
(breast portions halved)

1 celery stalk, chopped, with a few celery
leaves reserved for bouquet garni

1/2 large leek, chopped into thick chunks

1 medium onion, quartered

2 garlic cloves

12 baby carrots—4 whole, 8 halved
lengthwise

a bouquet garni (a bunch of herbs, such as
bay leaf, parsley, celery leaves and thyme,
tied together with kitchen twine)

1 teaspoon Quatre Epices
(European Spice Mixes, page 53))

1–1 1/2 tablespoons cornstarch

2/3 cup light cream (optional)

sea salt

Aromatic stock

1 lb. chicken bones and wings

3 bay leaves

1/2 cinnamon stick

8 whole cloves

1 onion, halved, with roots still attached

salt

Serves 4

France's quatre épices, or "four spices," is a popular blend of cloves, nutmeg, cinnamon, and pepper. Sometimes ginger or allspice may also appear. Quatre épices is used with chicken and pork in stews and terrines. France has a love of aromatics—think of saffron in bouillabaisse, juniper berries with meats, especially pork, cloves in onions (as in this stock), and vanilla in desserts and pastries. Herbs are used even more often, sometimes combined with spices. The flavor of this dish comes from the aromatic homemade stock, slow cooking, subtle spicing, and delicate herbs—real comfort food.

To make the stock, put the chicken bones, bay leaves, and cinnamon into a large saucepan. Stick the cloves into the onion and add to the pan, then cover with 2 quarts water. Bring to a boil and skim off the foam that rises to the surface. Reduce the heat to low, partly cover with a lid, and let simmer very gently for 1–1 1/2 hours. Pour through a fine-meshed strainer, let cool slightly, then skim off the globules of fat by trailing a small piece of paper towel across the surface. Add salt to taste.

Melt the butter and oil in a flameproof casserole and add the chicken pieces, celery, leek, onion, garlic, and the 4 whole carrots. Turn to coat with the butter and simmer for several minutes. Add stock to cover (about 2 2/3 cups) and freeze any remaining stock for other dishes.

Add the bouquet garni and quatre épices, bring to a boil, then cover and transfer to a preheated oven and cook at 325°F for 20 minutes. Add the halved baby carrots and cook for a further 20–25 minutes or until the chicken is tender. To test, pierce with a skewer—the juices should run clear with no hint of pink. If not, return to the oven for 5–10 minutes, then test again.

Remove from the oven, carefully strain off the liquid into a saucepan, and skim off the fat. Bring the liquid to a boil and reduce by about half. Meanwhile, put the cornstarch into a small cup and beat in a little water until smooth and lump free. Add a little of the hot stock and beat immediately until smooth. Take the saucepan off the heat and beat in the cornstarch paste. Replace the pan over low heat, beating constantly. As the sauce is simmering, beat in the cream, if using. Simmer, beating a little, until the sauce has slightly thickened. Gently stir the sauce into the casserole. Discard the bouquet garni, reheat the casserole without boiling, then serve.

Note To save time, make the stock in advance. Store overnight in the refrigerator or freeze in batches, including one of 2 2/3 cups for this casserole.

italian pork tenderloin
with fennel and garlic

The Romans had an insatiable desire for spices. They used native fennel and coriander seeds and "exotic" spices such as black pepper. In his first century cookbook, Apicius mentions spice mixtures using fennel seeds, and fennel was part of the reverse spice trade. The Romans probably (either directly or via Arab middlemen) introduced the seed to India where it is now much used. Today, fennel is found in the fine Tuscan sausage finocchiona, and is partnered with other sausages and pork dishes all over Italy. Incidentally, the marriage of pork with spices such as fennel or coriander spread from Italy to England, proving especially popular during Elizabethan times.

2 pork tenderloins, about 1 lb. each, trimmed

Fennel and pepper seasoning

2 teaspoons fennel seeds

½ teaspoon coarse salt

5 black peppercorns

2 garlic cloves, crushed

⅓ cup extra virgin olive oil

Serves 4

There are two ways to cook the pork. If you're in a hurry, use the fast-roast method, a favorite with many modern cooks. I prefer the slow-cooking method, which keeps meat like pork moister and more tender. Instructions for both follow.

To make the seasoning, grind the fennel seeds, salt, and peppercorns with a mortar and pestle. Mash in the garlic and olive oil to form a paste. Make a few light slashes in each tenderloin and put onto a roasting tray. Rub the seasoning oil all over the pork and pour any remaining oil on top.

To fast-roast, cook on the middle shelf of a preheated oven at 425°F for 20 minutes, or until the internal temperature registers 150°F on an instant-read thermometer, or until there are no pink juices when you pierce the meat with a skewer. Baste the pork several times while roasting.

If following the slower method, cook in a preheated oven at 325°F for about 45 minutes or until done, as above. Baste several times. For both methods, rest the pork for 10 minutes before serving, then slice and serve.

vanilla poached pears

Fruits and spices have long been deemed appropriate partners; think apples and cinnamon, mango and ginger, or pickling spices for fruit chutneys like plum or apricot.

Delicately poached fruits such as plums, peaches, and pears with vanilla or other "sweet" spices are part of the French culinary repertoire. Today this combination is evident in much of Europe, a Gallic gift bestowed on the rest of the Continent, just like the classical skills and refinement of the French kitchen. Choose firm pears that will hold up well, and serve with homemade vanilla ice cream.

8 small pears, slightly underripe

1 lemon, halved

1 bottle sweet white wine (750 ml), such as Moscatel de Valencia

3–4 tablespoons sugar or vanilla sugar*

1 vanilla bean, split lengthwise with a small, sharp knife*

Serves 4

*To make vanilla sugar, put a vanilla bean or beans into a glass container, cover with sugar, and seal. The beans can be dried after each use and returned to the container.

Using a vegetable peeler, peel the pears but leave the stem intact. Hold the pears over a bowl as you work and rub the lemon half and its juice over the fruit to prevent discoloration. To achieve a smooth surface, rub the pears with a clean dish towel and rub again with the lemon.

Put the wine into a stainless steel or enamel (non-reactive) saucepan, just big enough to hold the pears, stems upward. Add the sugar and 1/2 cup water and heat, stirring until the sugar dissolves. Add the split vanilla bean, pears, and lemon juice. Simmer gently for about 10 minutes, until the pears are tender but still firm. Remove with a slotted spoon and transfer to a serving bowl.

Boil the poaching liquid vigorously and reduce by half until syrupy, about 10 minutes. (Scrape the sides of the pan while the liquid is boiling so all the vanilla flecks stay in the liquid.)

Pour the syrup and vanilla bean over the fruits. Let cool and serve at room temperature or chilled, with vanilla ice cream.

Variations I use vanilla only, so its full glory scents the pears. You can, however, use combinations of other spices such as cinnamon, cloves, star anise, or even pepper.

bara brith speckled bread

I lived in an ancient Welsh village for eight years, and I've seen Welsh baking at its best. There was no shortage of neighbors and friends (especially octogenarian Auntie Bet) to show me how to make bara brith. Rich and sweetly spiced, the name means "speckled bread" and was traditionally made with leftover dough "speckled" with currants. Mixed spice is often called pudding spice or sweet spice and reflects the centuries-long British love of spices.

1¾ cups mixed dried fruit, such as raisins, currants, and citrus peel, about 10 oz.*

1¼ cups hot black tea

2¼ cups all-purpose flour

2 teaspoons baking powder

1¼–1½ teaspoons Mixed Spice (European Spice Mixes, page 52)

1 stick unsalted butter, melted, plus extra for serving

¾ cup sugar or light brown sugar

½–1 teaspoon molasses, for coloring

1 egg, beaten

2 lb. loaf pan lined with wax paper

Makes 1 large loaf

See note on dough and batter, page 4.

*Most packages of mixed fruit are sweetened with sugar and glucose syrup. If you use an unsweetened mix, you may like to add slightly more sugar to the recipe.

Put the fruit into a bowl, add the hot tea, let soak for at least 30 minutes, then drain the fruit and reserve the tea.

Put the flour, baking powder, and mixed spice into a large bowl and mix well. Put the melted butter into a separate bowl, add the reserved tea, sugar, and molasses and mix well. Add the beaten egg and fruit and mix again.

Pour the fruit mixture gradually into the flour and mix well into a wet dough. Pour the dough into the prepared loaf pan and bake on the middle shelf of a preheated oven at 325°F for about 1 hour 15 minutes, or until a skewer inserted into the center comes out clean and the top is evenly brown. Bara brith should be dark and moist—be careful towards the end of baking as the top can scorch easily.

Remove from the oven and transfer to a wire rack. Let cool a little before serving. Cut thick slices, spread them with butter, then serve with a proper cup of tea—a perfect afternoon interlude.

swedish lussekatter

1 stick unsalted butter, melted

1¼ cups milk

a large pinch of saffron threads
(about ¾ teaspoon), toasted in a
dry skillet, then crumbled

½ cup sugar

2 eggs, beaten separately

3¼ cups all-purpose flour,
plus extra for dusting

½ teaspoon salt

2 packages active dry yeast (¼ oz. each)

2 large baking trays, well greased

pastry brush

Makes 14

Saffron buns known as lussekatter (Lucia cats) are innately Swedish, made for the St Lucia's Day festival on 13th December. On this day, a procession is led by the prettiest maiden. She wears a white gown with red sash, and a crown of candles and lingonberry. Saffron, though always imported these days, used to be grown in southern Sweden.

Put the melted butter into a bowl, stir in the milk, saffron, sugar, and 1 of the beaten eggs. Set aside.

Put the flour and salt into a large bowl, mix briefly, then stir in the yeast. Gradually stir in the liquid mixture and knead into a shiny, soft, somewhat sticky dough. Cover with a damp dish towel and let rise in a warm place for about 45 minutes until doubled in size.

Knead the dough again: if it is too sticky, dust with flour as you knead. Divide into 14 pieces, roll into balls, then roll each ball into 8-inch lengths. Coil tightly into S-shapes, then arrange well apart on the baking trays. Cover and let rise in a warm place for 1¼ hours. During the last 15 minutes of rising time, preheat the oven to 425°F.

Using a pastry brush, glaze the tops with the remaining beaten egg. Bake in the preheated oven for 10–12 minutes until golden brown. Serve with coffee or gløgg.

gløgg—mulled wine

1 bottle fruity red wine (750 ml)

2 oz. fresh ginger, sliced
(about 7 thick slices)

1 cinnamon stick

8 whole cloves

½ teaspoon cardamom seeds (not pods)

3 tablespoons sugar, or to taste

4 teaspoons blanched almonds

4 teaspoons raisins

Serves 4 (makes about 3 cups)

Gløgg (Danish/Norwegian), glögg (Swedish/Icelandic), or glögi (Finnish) is essentially mulled wine, made throughout Scandinavia at Christmas and served in cups with almonds and raisins—a rich, complex flavor. Enjoy this drink with lussekatter or other pâtisserie.

Pour the wine into a saucepan and add the ginger, cinnamon, cloves, cardamom, and sugar. Warm gently for 10 minutes so that the spices infuse. Just before you are ready to serve, heat until almost boiling, reduce the heat, and simmer gently for 5 minutes. Divide the almonds and raisins between 4 cups. Add the gløgg and serve hot with spoons for scooping up the almonds and raisins.

plum chutney

Chutney, a cherished sweet and spicy condiment on the British table, is an Anglo-Indian remnant from the days of the East India Company and the Raj. Some of the commercial sweet chutneys are still sold under typically colonial brand names like Major Grey. Homemade versions, however, have always been popular in England – just another aspect of the national taste for jams and pickles to serve with bread, cheese and cold meats. They have acquired a distinctively British flavour, different from their originals in India. Though some sweet chutneys are made there, in fact authentic Indian chutneys are often more akin to relishes. The fresh coconut and lentil varieties of South India, for example, are freshly made for each meal.

1¾ lb. plums, about 14, pitted and chopped

8 oz. raisins, about 1⅓ cups

1 large onion, chopped

½ teaspoon salt

⅔ cup cider vinegar

1 recipe Pickling Spices
(European Spice Mixes, page 53),
in a spice ball or tied up in cheesecloth

½ teaspoon ground ginger

a good pinch of freshly grated nutmeg

¾ cup sugar or light brown sugar

*2 preserving jars with non-metal lids,
2 cups each, sterilized in a low oven*

2 wax disks

Makes about 1 quart

Put the plums, raisins, onion, and salt into a stainless steel preserving pan or heavy saucepan and add the vinegar. Stir, then add the ball or bag of pickling spices. Bring to a boil, reduce the heat, and simmer gently for about 40 minutes, stirring occasionally. Be careful not to scorch the chutney as it cooks and thickens.

Add the ginger, nutmeg, and sugar and mix well. Keep a close eye on the chutney and cook for another 10–15 minutes, stirring regularly to make sure it doesn't burn. It should be dark and tangy yet sweet and thick. As it cools and sets, it will become thicker still.

Remove the ball or bag of pickling spices and pour the chutney into the sterilized jar(s) while still hot. Line the lid(s) with wax paper and seal the jar(s).

Note To make chutney, use a stainless steel pan, not copper, which will react with the vinegar. Seal the top of the chutney with wax disks and use non-metal lids (vinegar will corrode metal). For extra information on preserving, see page 4. For useful information on preserving, see website http://hgic.clemson.edu/factsheets/HGIC3040.htm

european spice mixes

It was perhaps because Europe's own native spices are few in number—dill, fennel, caraway, and coriander seeds, and juniper berries—that it became such a market for everyone else's. In the past, spices that are difficult to come by today, such as cubeb, grains of paradise, long pepper, and galangal, were more readily available. Early spice blends from France and Italy often incorporated such spice gems.

Mixed Spice

For most who think of English food as plain, it is interesting to note that the English have used spices to varying degrees for at least 1500 years, in both sweet and savory dishes. Mixed spice is used in cakes, breads, and desserts and is similar to America's Apple Pie Spice and Pumpkin Pie Spice. Nutmeg and mace, both from the same tree, are essentials in this mixture.

¼ cinnamon stick

1 teaspoon whole cloves (about 20)

2 blades of mace, or 1 teaspoon ground

¾ teaspoon freshly grated nutmeg

Grind the spices together to a fine powder and store in an airtight container. A common variation is to add a few allspice berries.

Scandinavian Mulling Spices

A popular way to spice wine in many parts of Northern Europe. Gløgg (see page 49), the Danish/Norwegian version, requires cardamom, cloves, cinnamon, and ginger. For a mild mulled wine, use cinnamon, cloves, allspice, and a few optional peppercorns. In the 17th century, when unusual spices were much more common in Europe, grains of paradise were used.

Pickling Spices

This spice combination is typical of those used in Britain to make pickles and chutneys. Other spices, such as chiles, mace, and occasionally dill seeds, could also be included.

1½ teaspoons coriander seeds

1 teaspoon allspice berries

½ teaspoon whole cloves (about 10)

¼ teaspoon black peppercorns

¾ teaspoon mustard seeds (yellow or brown)

Tie the spices in a cheesecloth bag or put in a meshed spice ball. Suspend in the pickle or chutney while it is cooking or, if spicing vinegar, put directly into the vinegar and leave to infuse before straining and using.

Quatre Épices

This French blend means "four spices." It usually contains the spices in this recipe, but it can also include ginger or allspice. The mixture is used to flavor soups, stews, vegetables, and the famous French spiced bread, or *pain d'épices*.

½ teaspoon whole cloves (about 10)

1 cinnamon stick

¼ teaspoon black peppercorns

1 teaspoon freshly grated nutmeg

Grind the whole spices to a fine powder, then mix in the grated nutmeg. Store in an airtight container.

Early English Ginger and Saffron

According to Elizabeth David in *Spices, Salt, and Aromatics in the English Kitchen*, many 15th-century recipes for spice mixes included ginger or saffron. Two are quoted as "cannelle [cinnamon], pepir, gyngere, and safroun" and "wyne, gyngere, pepir, and safroun."

Early Neapolitan Spice Blend

This recipe is adapted from *El Libro de Guisados, Manjares y Potajes* (1529) by Ruperto de Nola, cook to the King of Naples.

1 cinnamon stick

1 teaspoon whole cloves (about 20)

½ teaspoon black peppercorns

a pinch of saffron threads

½ teaspoon ground ginger

¼ teaspoon ground coriander

Grind the whole spices together to a fine powder and mix in the ginger and coriander. Store in an airtight container.

MUSTARDS

Prepared mustards have been enjoyed in Europe for hundreds of years; I've even found a recipe in my reprinted copy of Robert May's 1660 book, *The Accomplisht Cook*. Germany, France, and England (and America) all have their own mustards, and modern versions with extra spices abound.

French Dijon is, perhaps, everyone's favorite; always refined and more mellow than some of the pungently strong mustards to be found elsewhere. Dijon has been renowned for its mustard for more than 600 years—and the town still produces a gargantuan amount. Dijon mustard is pale and smooth, made from brown mustard seeds, spices, and white wine. The French also blend mustards with Champagne and red wine, and flavor them with honey, sugar, and herbs such as tarragon; styles vary from smooth to coarse.

English Very fierce in strength and bright yellow; made using mustard "meale" (powder) and water.

American Also bright in color, but not nearly as strong as English mustard; always visible at hot dog stands and backyard barbecues.

German mustard I've eaten many a bratwurst with this mustard; light and lively with herbs and spices.

Wholegrain mustard A coarse-textured mustard in which the seeds are cracked but not blended until smooth, producing a very satisfying texture.

Other mustards Hot mustards are spiced with chiles, herb mustards are flavored with various herbs. Honey mustard is very popular in the States and is made using vinegar and honey.

africa and the middle east

The Middle East and Africa comprise a vast area, with a history as old as time. It is to this region that we owe the birth of civilization, and it was the Arabs who first drove their camel caravans along the incense route and made early sea voyages in search of spices. Three thousand years ago, the Phoenicians (from today's Lebanon and Syria) and Sabeans (from Sheba, today's Yemen) distributed aromatics and spices from the East Indies and China, along with indigenous spices from all around the Mediterranean.

A visit to the souks in the Gulf States will reveal lanes lined with hessian sacks of every imaginable spice—roots, seeds, and barks from near and far. Fenugreek and coriander grown around the Mediterranean vie for attention with cloves from Zanzibar, vanilla from Madagascar, nutmeg from Indonesia, and cardamom from India. The great Spice Bazaars of Istanbul (former Constantinople) and Cairo are as large, brilliant, and bustling as they have ever been.

The culinary imprint of past cultures and history is evident everywhere. The ancient Egyptians brought cinnamon from Punt (modern Somalia); the Persians contributed subtly spiced food scented with saffron, cardamom, and rosewater, thickened with nuts and sweetened with dried fruits; while the fiery imprint of chiles shows the contribution of the seafaring Portuguese.

incense, spice, and arabian nights

If there were ever a story laden with all the mystique of the Arabian Nights, it is the tale of the spice trade in the Middle East and the Horn of Africa.

Spice use in the region dates back to the world's earliest written records and cultures—to Ancient Mesopotamia (modern Iraq), often referred to as the "cradle of civilization"—where spices were used as food, medicine, and perfume. In Mesopotamia, one of the earliest written poems, the *Epic of Gilgamesh*, tells of royal banquets where guests were presented with herbs and perfumes of ginger as a pre-dinner gift. The Bible gives an account of the Ishmaelites buying Joseph on their way from Gilead to Egypt laden with "spicery, balm, and myrrh," and describes coriander as "like manna from heaven."

The Queen of Sheba's visit to King Solomon was described in the First Book of Kings and the Second Book of Chronicles: "She came to Jerusalem with a very great retinue, with camels bearing spices and very much gold, and precious stones ..." It is to her shimmering kingdom of Saba (Sheba) and neighboring city-states (now in Yemen) that we mostly owe the spread of spices east and west.

The ports of Hadramant and Aden capitalized on the monsoon winds to carry Yemeni merchants across the Indian Ocean.

By the first century AD, Pliny the Elder said the incense trade had made the people of Southern Arabia the richest on earth. Much of their wealth came from two enviable commodities—frankincense and myrrh, only to be found in Yemen, southern Oman, and parts of Somalia. Donkey and camel caravans traveled great distances along the incense route bearing these aromatic resins, and also spices, textiles, and other goods to Mesopotamia, Greece, and Rome.

There is much evidence of the existence of ancient maritime trading routes bearing spices and textiles from India, silk from China, and gold and ostrich feathers from the Horn of Africa. These routes led from Indonesia, Sri Lanka, and India across to Arabia.

In Ancient Egypt, spices such as cumin, coriander, aniseed, fennel, juniper, fenugreek, and poppy seeds, documented in the medical treatise the *Codex Eburs*, were used for cooking, making scent and in embalming rituals.

Dates for many of the events of this most remarkable of civilizations are often disputed, but it is known that between 2000–1000 BC, Egyptians were traveling the incense route to the Horn of Africa to the land called Punt (now Somalia) to procure frankincense and myrrh as well as Eastern spices, including prized cassia and cinnamon.

By 1380 BC, the slaves of Pharaoh Amenhotep III finished building a canal that connected the Nile with the Red Sea, allowing spices and other trade goods to be brought more easily to the center of the Egyptian world—this over 3000 years before the Suez Canal did the same for our world.

Meanwhile, old and new overland routes, like the Silk Road, continued to be used to exchange incense, spices, silk, gold, and gems. The Silk Road famously wound its way from Babylon through much of Persia and Central Asia, finally reaching China with an offshoot to the Indus Valley in Pakistan.

Ancient Persia (now Iran), which so influenced the cookery of the Middle East, North Africa, India, and Pakistan, was in a central position along these routes. Persian saffron conquered both the Middle East and India with its golden hue, exchanged for Indian spices such as cardamom, spreading their use through Persia's vast empire.

Other ancient Middle Eastern and North African civilizations became great

trading societies, particularly the Phoenicians, operating from the city of Tyre, in what is now Lebanon, and their western outpost in Carthage (modern Tunisia), they distributed spices around the eastern and western Mediterranean, and further afield.

Worth its weight in gold, all this mercantile knowledge and trading partnerships with powerful civilizations, gleaned over centuries, meant that the Arabs remained wealthy middlemen for a very long time. Not only did they control the flow of goods from East to West, but they also became fiercely protective of the source of these goods. Inevitably, others would want to cash in on the lucrative trade.

In the first century AD, the Romans rediscovered the effects of the monsoon winds that had created the spice wealth of Sheba and the Arabs began to lose their dominance. Then, though sea routes continued to exist, the fall of the Chinese Han Dynasty in the third century signaled the closure of the Silk Road, reducing east-west trade to a fraction of what it had been.

When Islam swept the Middle East in the seventh century, the Arabs rose

again to take huge swathes of territory from South Asia to Spain. The Moors of North Africa conquered Spain, taking with them spices like cinnamon, cumin, and saffron, which is still grown near La Mancha. Medieval Egypt once again controlled the trade routes, extending its reach all the way to Guinea and Mali in West Africa, and as far as Java across the Indian Ocean.

The Dark Ages overwhelmed Europe at the same time as the Golden Age of Islam brought riches, poetry, and learning to the Caliphate of Baghdad— and spices went hand in hand with the Caliphs' love of all things sophisticated. The saffron, nuts, cardamom, fruits, and scented waters taken from the Persian court, along with Eastern spices, permeated medieval Arab cooking. From elaborate rice dishes to scented meat and fruit stews, the rulers and their retinues ate in exalted fashion. In the 13th century Baghdad cookery book, *Kitab-al-Tabiikh*, spice mixtures abound, and a thoughtful preamble suggesting how to choose, grind, and use spices is astonishing in its complexity. A divine recipe called *manbusha* asks the cook to "Add brayed (crushed) pepper, cinnamon, and mastic (a fruity resin) to the cooked meat, garnish with poached eggs,

sprinkle with fine brayed cinnamon, and spray with a little rosewater ... Leave over the fire an hour to settle."

Several centuries later, the great European powers were determined to break the iron grip of spice monopoly held by the Venetians and their Arab partners (page 36). Columbus set off westward in search of the Indies and the Portuguese Vasco da Gama found the route around the Cape of Good Hope to India and the Spice Islands. The Arab-Venetian monopoly was truly shattered as the Portuguese, Dutch, English—even the Danes—set up trading empires in the east.

Yet, with a spice history of such mythical proportions, it comes as no surprise that today's Middle Eastern and North African cooking is still rich with spices. A veritable Aladdin's cave of aromatic dishes reveals the region's age-old connection with spices, scents, and trade in rich and rare goods.

__Above, from left__: Sand dunes near Siwa Oasis near the Egyptian/Libyan border, one of the life-saving watering points on the desert caravan routes of North Africa • Camel market in a village outside Luxor, Egypt • Cairo's Spice Bazaar, one of the great markets of the world • Istanbul's Spice Bazaar.

tomato and lentil salad
adis ma bandoora

Lentils are an important source of protein throughout the Middle East and Africa, as they are in Asia and parts of the Mediterranean. This salad is from Lebanon and Syria, but similar lentil dishes can be found from Jordan to Egypt and Turkey. Sumac* is an indispensable Middle Eastern spice and used as a souring agent. Other spices particularly popular in the Levant include caraway and allspice.

1 cup brown lentils (about 7 oz.)

5 tablespoons extra virgin olive oil

1 medium onion, halved and finely sliced

1 lb. cherry tomatoes, about 30, quartered

2 teaspoons sumac, plus extra to serve*

sea salt and freshly ground black pepper

Serves 4–6

Put the lentils into a bowl, cover with plenty of cold water, and soak for 2 hours or according to the instructions on the package. Drain, transfer to a saucepan, add a pinch of salt, and cover with boiling water. Return to a boil, reduce the heat, and simmer for 15 minutes or until *al dente* (tender but still firm). Drain well and set aside.

Clean the pan, add 2 tablespoons of the oil, heat well, then add the onion. Sauté gently for about 8 minutes until softened and translucent. Remove from the heat and add the lentils, tomatoes, sumac, salt, pepper, and the remaining 3 tablespoons oil. Stir gently with a wooden spoon and serve as a side dish, with extra sumac served separately.

*Note If you can't find sumac but would like to try this salad, opt for a completely different flavor, but still Middle Eastern. In the Levant, caraway is used in many ways, and will give this salad a light anise flavor rather than the sour edge provided by the sumac. Add 1 teaspoon caraway seeds when you heat the oil, then proceed with the recipe—a refreshing alternative.

african seafood kebabs
with piri piri basting oil

12 large, uncooked shrimp, peeled, but with tail fins intact

8–12 small sea scallops, muscles removed

12–20 bay leaves

ciabatta or focaccia bread, to serve

Piri piri basting oil

3 garlic cloves, crushed

5–6 red bird's eye chiles or 8–9 regular red chiles, seeded and coarsely chopped

freshly squeezed juice of $\frac{1}{2}$ lemon

$\frac{1}{3}$–$\frac{1}{2}$ cup extra virgin olive oil

$\frac{1}{2}$ teaspoon nigella seeds (optional)

4 metal skewers

Serves 4

The piri piri is a fiercely hot variety of chile introduced to Africa by the Portuguese, probably via Western India. The name is also used for the hot sauces in which the pods are used. Versions of piri piri sauce can be found in many former Portuguese colonies, from Mozambique and Angola to Brazil, as well as Portugal itself. In Southern Africa, piri piri chiles are a commercial crop, and there is even a South African restaurant chain marketing its own brand of piri piri sauce, now widely available in other parts of the world. For this recipe, use any hot, thin red chiles—they don't have to be piri piri. Although nigella seeds are not a traditional component, they add a flavor and texture to this dish that I like very much. Although more commonly identified with Indian cookery, nigella (also called kalonji) is also popular in East Africa.

To make the piri piri basting oil, put the garlic, chiles, lemon juice and olive oil into a blender and blend until smooth. Transfer to a bowl and stir in the nigella seeds, if using.

Dip the shrimp and scallops into the basting oil and coat well. Thread the shrimp and scallops alternately onto the skewers, with the bay leaves between them.

Set apart on a broiler rack over a broiler tray. Cook at high heat under a preheated broiler for about 5 minutes or until done, turning once during cooking. (Don't overcook or the scallops will be tough—shrimp and scallops are done when the flesh becomes opaque.) Brush with the piri piri basting oil several times while the skewers are cooking. Alternatively, put the remaining oil into a small saucepan, boil for 1–2 minutes, then serve as a dipping sauce.

moroccan grilled fish
with chermoula spice paste

Chermoula is a spicy Moroccan sauce or marinade for fish. In dilapidated but bustling Tangier, huge baskets of spices and herbs, such as the cilantro and cumin for chermoula, are lined up for sale in the souks. The color of this sauce is produced by fresh cilantro, while the chili powder gives it a kick. It can be used as both a marinade and a topping.

4 steaks of tuna, or swordfish, about 7–8 oz. each, lightly scored

sea salt and freshly ground black pepper

extra virgin olive oil, for cooking

cilantro, to serve

Chermoula

a few handfuls of cilantro leaves and stems, coarsely chopped

3 garlic cloves, chopped

1/4 teaspoon sweet pimentón (Spanish oak-smoked paprika)

1/2 teaspoon ground cumin

1/2 teaspoon chili powder

1/4 cup extra virgin olive oil

freshly squeezed juice of 1/2 lemon

sea salt

a stove-top grill pan

Serves 4

To make the chermoula, put the cilantro and garlic into a blender or food processor. Add the paprika, cumin, chili powder, olive oil, lemon juice, and a pinch of salt and blend to a smooth paste—if necessary, add a dash of water to let the blades run. Alternatively, use a mortar and pestle.

About 30 minutes before cooking the fish, sprinkle it with salt, put a spoonful of chermoula onto each steak and rub all over. Set aside to marinate.

When ready to cook, brush a stove-top grill pan with olive oil and heat over medium-high heat until very hot. Add the fish to the pan and cook for 1–2 minutes, depending on thickness. Don't move the fish until it loosens and will move without sticking. Turn it over and continue cooking for 1–2 minutes If the fish is very thick, cook for 1 minute longer, but do not overcook or the flesh will be tough. (If you have a small pan, cook in batches of 1 or 2 and keep them warm in a very low oven while you cook the remainder.)

Top each piece of fish with the remaining chermoula and serve with extra cilantro.

Note If you would like to serve the fish with typical North African accompaniments, roast some butternut squash or sweet potatoes with olive oil and cinnamon, and make some fluffy couscous, with a little saffron added to the soaking water.

lamb and apricot tagine

1/2 teaspoon ground turmeric

1/2 teaspoon ground ginger

2 lb. boned shoulder of lamb, well trimmed of fat and cut into large chunks

2 tablespoons unsalted butter

2 medium onions, chopped

1/2 cinnamon stick

1 tablespoon Ras el Hanout (African and Middle Eastern Spice Mixes, page 72)

1 tomato, peeled and chopped

1 teaspoon honey (optional)

6 oz. dried apricots, halved

sea salt

To serve

steamed couscous

a few cilantro leaves

2 tablespoons sesame seeds, toasted in a dry skillet

1–2 tablespoons argan oil (optional)*

Serves 4

Argan oil is extracted from the nuts of Morocco's argan tree, and is said to be even healthier than the best olive oil. The trees, once common, have been dying out, but efforts are now being made to re-establish them. The oil is expensive because it takes 60 lb. of nuts to produce 1 quart. It is used in dips, on its own, or in dressings. It is sometimes available specialty shops and is definitely worth trying if you see it for sale.

Used in North African cooking, ras el hanout is one of the most intricate spice blends, and it is all the more alluring for its mystery. On a recent visit to Morocco, I marveled as spice merchants blended their own secret recipes, adding all manner of spices, flower petals, roots, bark, and aphrodisiacs like Spanish fly! Unusual spices are sometimes included, such as locally popular cubeb, grains of paradise, monk's pepper, ash berries, long pepper, galangal, and occasionally nigella. Something about ras el hanout evokes the image of the genie and his magic! If you can find cold-pressed argan oil, it gives the tagine a nutty finishing touch.

A few hours before making the tagine, put the turmeric and ginger into a bowl, mix well, then rub into the lamb. Cover and set aside to develop the flavors.

Melt the butter in a heavy saucepan or casserole and add the onions, cinnamon, lamb, ras el hanout, and salt. Mix well, then add the chopped tomato, honey, if using, and 2 cups water. Bring to a boil, then reduce the heat to low and simmer gently, partly covered with a lid, for 45 minutes, stirring occasionally. Uncover and simmer for a further 45 minutes, stirring occasionally.

Add the apricots and simmer gently for 25 minutes. When ready, the sauce should just coat the lamb all over, rich and almost glaze-like. Remove from the heat. Serve hot with couscous and sprinkle with cilantro, sesame seeds, and a little argan oil, if using.

*Argan oil is extracted from the nuts of Morocco's argan tree, and is said to be even healthier than the best olive oil. The trees, once common, have been dying out, but efforts are now being made to re-establish them. The oil is rare and expensive because it takes 60 lb. of nuts to extract 1 quart. It is used in dips, on its own, or in dressings. It is sometimes available specialty stores and definitely worth trying if you see it for sale.

Note A tagine is a slow-cooked stew that takes its name from the conical earthenware pot in which it is traditionally cooked. Avoid the urge to raise the heat and cook the lamb quickly, as the slow simmering over low heat is responsible for the tagine's tenderness and for reducing the sauce to a rich coating.

lamb kabob mashwi
with spiced flatbreads

1½ lb. trimmed, boneless leg of lamb, twice-ground (ask the butcher to put the meat through the grinder twice)

1 large onion, finely chopped

1 teaspoon sea salt

¼ cup chopped fresh marjoram

2 tablespoons chopped fresh mint

2 teaspoons Baharat (African and Middle Eastern Spice Mixes, page 72)

1 teaspoon loomi (dried lime) powder, (optional)*

Mafrouda (spiced flatbreads)

3½ cups white bread flour

1 package (¼ oz.) active dry yeast

1 teaspoon sea salt

¼ teaspoon sugar

1 tablespoon extra virgin olive oil

2 teaspoons Zahtar (African and Middle Eastern Spice Mixes, page 73)

To serve

2 shallots, sliced and soaked in lemon juice

1 tablespoon chopped mint

thick plain yogurt mixed with a little tahini paste

sumac, to sprinkle (optional)

2 large baking trays

Serves 4

See note on dough and batter, page 4.

In the Arabian Gulf States, where many kinds of kabobs are popular (even dates are cooked on skewers), kabob mashwi is one of the most delicious. This recipe uses a number of regional spices and also includes herbs. Kabobs are usually served with flatbreads wherever you find them, from India to North Africa. In these areas, people eat with their fingers, so the bread is used to pull the kabobs off the skewers.

To make the flatbreads, preheat the oven to 425°F. Put the flour into a large bowl, make a well in the center, and add the yeast. Gradually add enough tepid water to make a pliable dough, about 1 cup. Start bringing the flour into the center. Add the salt, sugar, and oil and knead well for 5 minutes. Add the zahtar and continue kneading for 5 minutes. Although this is leavened bread, the dough should not rest. Form into 4 balls and roll out into long rectangular shapes or rounds. Prick the flatbreads all over with a fork. Arrange on baking trays and bake for about 2 minutes, then turn them over and cook for a further 2 minutes. Serve warm. (To keep the breads warm, wrap in foil or a dish towel until ready to serve.)

To make the kabobs, put the lamb, onion, salt, marjoram, mint, *baharat,* and loomi*, if using, into a large bowl. Mix well with your hands. Form into 12 egg shapes and push onto skewers. Alternatively, shape the lamb around the skewers. Put the kabobs onto a lightly greased rack under a preheated broiler and cook for about 8 minutes or until done. Alternatively, prepare an outdoor grill and brush the rack with a little oil so that the kabobs don't stick. Grill at medium heat for 5 minutes or until nicely browned, turning frequently to cook evenly.

Ask guests to assemble the kabobs themselves—use the flatbread as a base, add shallots and mint, then the kabobs, yogurt with tahini, and a sprinkle of sumac, if using.

*Note Loomi are dried limes, available in Middle Eastern stores. Most come from Oman, and are used both whole and in powdered form throughout the Gulf States. Traditionally, limes are buried in the sand for a few months to dry or can be dried in the sun for at least a week. The spice is difficult to emulate, though you can omit it. You could, however, try drying a few pierced limes in the oven (which takes ages!) or the microwave. When dried, you can grind them to a powder.

perfumed persian pulow

1/2 teaspoon ground cinnamon

1/4 teaspoon ground cardamom
(preferably white, made only from the
seeds, not the pods)

1/2 teaspoon sugar

1/3 cup raisins, soaked in warm water
for 5 minutes

1/3 cup sliced almonds, toasted in a
dry skillet

1/4 cup shelled unsalted pistachios,
coarsely chopped

3/4 cup frozen peas, thawed and blanched
in boiling water

13/4 cups basmati rice

1 teaspoon sea salt

3 tablespoons extra virgin olive oil

1 tablespoon freshly grated orange zest

a large pinch of saffron threads,
soaked in 2 tablespoons hot water
and 2 tablespoons orange flower water

2 tablespoons clarified butter (ghee) or
melted regular butter, to serve

Serves 4–6

Iranians are undoubtedly the greatest rice cooks. Their sophisticated cuisine dates back to the ancient Persian Empire, which wooed its conquered lands with delicious food. Use only basmati for this dish, or it will disappoint, and follow the timings for the recipe. They work.

Mix the cinnamon, cardamom, and sugar in a small bowl and set aside. Mix the raisins, almonds, pistachios, and peas in a second bowl and set aside.

Put the rice into a strainer and rinse under cold running water until the water runs clear. Transfer to a large bowl, cover with fresh cold water, and soak for 2 hours. Drain well (never press the rice to drain—this damages the grains). Put about 5 cups water into a large saucepan, bring to a boil, add a pinch of salt, then the rice. Return to a boil and cook for 3–4 minutes without stirring. Drain well and rinse briefly in warm water.

Heat the oil in the same saucepan, then reduce the heat to the lowest possible. Add layers of ingredients in the following order (you will have 3–4 layers, depending on the size of the saucepan)—a layer of rice, a layer of the raisin-nut-and-pea mixture, a pinch of zest, and a pinch of the spice-and-sugar mixture. Repeat this layering pattern until all the ingredients have been used, and finishing with a layer of rice.

Sprinkle with the saffron and its soaking liquid. Using a the end of a wooden spoon, poke a few holes in the rice all the way down to the bottom of the pan. Cover tightly with a lid lined with a dish towel, so that no steam escapes. Cook over very low heat for about 20 minutes—or leave it on super-low for even longer, as Iranian cooks do.

When ready to serve, remove from the heat, lift the lid and towel, pour the clarified butter over the pulow, then fluff up with a fork. Serve hot with other dishes. (A delicious crust will have formed on the bottom of the pan—this is known as *tahdeeg* in Iran and it is the most coveted part of the rice!)

Note I rarely wash and soak rice, because it is unnecessary with modern methods of rice production and you lose some of the nutritional value of the rice when doing so. However, for special and traditional dishes, such as this one, which are prepared on rare occasions, this method is well worth the effort. The results are sublime, and the soaked rice cooks in a very short time. The method is also useful when using brown basmati as it softens the texture of the unrefined grains.

ricotta-stuffed dates
with spicy arab coffee

½ cup ricotta cheese

2 teaspoons superfine sugar

1 teaspoon freshly grated nutmeg

18 best quality dates, such as mozafati or medjool, pitted

Arab spiced coffee

4 heaping tablespoons best quality coarsely ground coffee

1½ teaspoons cardamom seeds, plus 4 whole cardamom pods, bruised

1 teaspoon rosewater or orange flower water

light brown sugar, to serve (optional)*

Serves 6

Arabs usually drink this coffee unsweetened. However, it tastes delicious with a little brown sugar, so serve it separately.

During our stint in Saudi Arabia, my husband and I delighted in stuffed dates and cardamom-laced Arab coffee. The latter was a symbol of Arab hospitality, served black and in tiny cups, with as many refills as you could handle. It is actually considered an insult to drink only one cup! Poured from elegant, long-spouted coffee pots with an extra cardamom pod wedged in the spout, the coffee comes out in a fragrant arc.

The indigenous date palm has long been essential throughout North Africa and the Middle East. In the arid climate and desert terrain, nomadic peoples from the Atlantic to the Persian Gulf could depend on this source of nourishment. Dates are often stuffed with local cheeses, but come into their own when stuffed with sweetly spiced ricotta. Find the best dates you can, for example mozafati (known as the king of dates) or medjool. And don't bother with ready-ground nutmeg in this recipe—it really must be freshly grated to taste as good as it should.

To prepare the dates, put the ricotta cheese into a small bowl and beat well. Add the sugar and nutmeg and mix until smooth. Stuff each date with a little of the spiced ricotta and serve on a small plate.

To make the coffee, put the ground coffee and cardamom into a large saucepan, then add 5 cups boiling water. (If you prefer even stronger coffee, use only 4 cups). Add the rosewater or orange flower water and return to a boil. Reduce the heat and simmer for 1 minute, then turn off the heat. Cover with a lid and set aside for about 30 minutes.

Before serving, gently warm the coffee without boiling and transfer to a heated coffee pot. Pour into small espresso or Arab coffee cups and serve.

spice mixes of africa and the middle east

Traders from these regions have provided spices to the world. The camel caravans, more than 3000 years ago, introduced the western world to the pleasure of spices, and even today the spice bazaars of Cairo, Morocco, and Istanbul are the stuff of romance.

Ras el Hanout

Mostly identified with Moroccan cooking, but found in other parts of North Africa, ras el hanout means "top of the store." It is a mixture that varies from store to store and cook to cook— a pinch of this and a pinch of that. The mixture below is a popular one, but you can vary it according to the flavors you like best—try turmeric, nigella, saffron, pepper, cardamom, coriander, cloves, lavender, and, if you can get them, ash berries, grains of paradise, or monk's pepper. It is used in many meat dishes and with rice and couscous.

1 teaspoon cardamom seeds (not pods)

1 blade of mace or ½ teaspoon ground mace (optional)

1 teaspoon cubeb (optional) or black peppercorns

3 allspice berries

½ cinnamon stick

a large pinch of saffron threads

1 teaspoon freshly grated nutmeg

1 teaspoon ground ginger

2–3 unsprayed dried rosebuds, torn into small pieces

Toast the whole spices in a dry skillet over low heat until aromatic. Take care

because they burn easily. Stir in the nutmeg, ginger, and rose petals. Store in an airtight container. Just before using, grind to a powder with a mortar and pestle.

Harissa

This very hot Tunisian spice paste can be bought in tubes and jars—or by the ladle in North African delicatessens. It has a smoky, fiery flavor and can be added to stews, grills, chickpeas, or other foods. It is also served as a condiment with couscous.

½ teaspoon caraway seeds

1½ teaspoons coriander seeds

¾ teaspoon cumin seeds

4–5 hot dried red chiles, seeded and soaked in warm water

1 garlic clove, crushed

3 tablespoons extra virgin olive oil

a pinch of sea salt

Toast the whole seeds in a dry skillet over low heat for a few minutes until aromatic. Grind coarsely, then transfer to a blender and add the chiles, garlic, oil, and salt. Blend to a thick paste and store in the refrigerator.

Zahtar

This simple blend is used to flavor breads and vegetables throughout the Middle East, but it is particularly popular in the Gulf, the Levant, Turkey, and North Africa.

1 tablespoon crushed dried thyme

1 tablespoon sumac

2 tablespoons lightly toasted sesame seeds.

Mix all the ingredients together. Store in an airtight container.

Hawayij

A peppery Yemeni blend which is also very popular in Israel, used to flavor meat, soups, and stews.

1 teaspoon black peppercorns
¼ teaspoon cardamom seeds (not pods)
½ teaspoon ground turmeric
a large pinch of saffron threads
½ teaspoon caraway seeds (optional)

Grind the ingredients to a fine powder and store in an airtight container.

Lebanese/Syrian Spice Mix

This recipe varies from one cook to another, but this is a rough guide. The mix is used to flavor soups and stews of meat or vegetables.

½ teaspoon cardamom pods
½ teaspoon chili powder
½ teaspoon ground cloves
1 teaspoon ground cinnamon

Grind the cardamom pods to a powder and mix in the ground spices. Store in an airtight container.

Baharat or Bezar

The major blend of the Gulf States. The spices vary slightly and the mix carries local names. As in other blends of the region, the Indian influence is strong.

1 small piece of cinnamon or cassia bark
½ teaspoon cardamom seeds (not pods)
1 teaspoon whole cloves (about 20)
½ teaspoon black peppercorns
1 teaspoon coriander seeds
½ teaspoon ground turmeric
about ¼ teaspoon freshly grated nutmeg
1½ teaspoons sweet pimentón (oak-smoked Spanish paprika)
¼ teaspoon chili powder

Grind the spices to a fine powder; if you like, you can toast them in a dry skillet first. Store in an airtight container.

Ethiopian Berbere

This mixture from the Horn of Africa is similar to roasted South Indian masalas, requires fenugreek, chiles, and coriander, but the other spices may vary slightly from home to home. It is used in wats (traditional Ethiopian stews).

1 teaspoon fenugreek seeds
10 medium-to-large dried red chiles
1 teaspoon coriander seeds
1 teaspoon cardamom seeds (not pods)
5 black peppercorns
5 whole cloves
2 small pieces of cinnamon or cassia
2 teaspoons ground ginger

Roast the whole spices in a dry skillet over low heat for a few minutes, until aromatic. Grind to a fine powder. Add the ginger and blend well. Store in an airtight container.

Egyptian Dukka

A strongly flavored spicy nut mix used throughout the Eastern Mediterranean. It is eaten with bread as an appetizer or dry dip and is also good sprinkled into yogurt or over salads. I've added just a dash of sugar to soften it, but you could leave it out for authenticity. For a more fiery dukka, add hot red pepper flakes.

½ cup shelled hazelnuts, chopped
¼ cup sesame seeds
¼ cup cumin seeds
½ teaspoon dried marjoram
¼ teaspoon dried thyme
½ teaspoon freshly grated lemon zest
a pinch of light brown sugar (optional)
sea salt and freshly ground black pepper

Put the nuts and seeds into a dry skillet and toast until aromatic. Add the remaining ingredients and store in an airtight container.

south asia

Could we possibly imagine South Asia without spices? The natural home of these desirable exotics, the Indian subcontinent lured merchants on perilous journeys from antiquity to medieval times. The peppercorns of the southern Malabar coast, in particular, were once more expensive than gold, inspiring everyone from the Romans to the British to seek out the prized berries. Spices cannot be divorced from the region's soul, so integral are they to the native psyche and diet. Green and black cardamom, peppercorns, cinnamon, cassia, turmeric, asafoetida, tamarind, and more—an astounding cornucopia of native seasonings greets the eye in the market and even the medicine cabinet. The briefest visit to India, Pakistan, Nepal, Bangladesh, Sri Lanka, Afghanistan, or the Indian Ocean islands will leave your tastebuds tingling.

The most important elements of spice use are the tarka (spice-fry) and the ground masala (spice blend). There are as many masalas as there are households: each is a careful regional blend based on thousands of years of local practice, and everyone takes pride in their own discrete version. Although ready-made blends are commonplace even in South Asia, most families grind whole spices to make their own blends—and, of course, no self-respecting housewife uses anything like "curry powder."

Spices used vary from north to south, east to west—and you may find some dishes to be extremely delicate, while in others the spices leap out. The very art of South Asian cooking is in getting this balance just right.

indian spices: from the romans to the raj

Although the story of spices in South Asia is irreversibly tied to the Portuguese conquest of India's southwestern Malabar Coast, land and sea spice routes existed long before Vasco da Gama stepped ashore in Calicut in 1498 crying out, "For Christians and spices."

From ancient times, India has held an irresistible allure for the rest of the world as the source of coveted spices. Steeped in a history as old as the first civilizations of Egypt and Mesopotamia, the Indian subcontinent is the home of myriad spices luring merchants from near and far.

Many of these spices grow wild (and in carefully managed plantations) in the lush Cardamom Hills, inland from the Malabar Coast. Even today, spices are a way of life in this region, and many people nurture their own small spice gardens, with pepper vines rambling casually through the trees. Exquisitely scented cinnamon originated in Sri Lanka, but was naturalized in Kerala long ago; saffron and asafoetida (both introduced from Persia) prosper in Kashmir; while mustard, although grown throughout the subcontinent, is produced in great commercial quantities in Nepal.

Evidence of early *yavanas* or foreigners seeking spices in return for various commodities comes in many forms; Greek pottery, Roman coins, and Chinese fishing nets in Malabar and Coromandel ports all stand as proof. Even earlier, around 3000 BC the great Indus Valley city of Harappa had established maritime trade with its contemporary, the city of Sumer in Mesopotamia. The traffic wasn't all one way, either—spices native to the Mediterranean, such as coriander, cumin, fennel, and saffron, asafoetida from Persia, and cloves, nutmeg, and star anise from the Spice Islands and China were used in the subcontinent thousands of years ago. However, the arrival of the chile had to wait awhile ...

Ancient land routes led merchants through what is now Afghanistan and Pakistan, to Delhi, Varanasi, and other important cities along the Ganges. Other major cities were connected to this route by arterial roads. In the south, similar routes linked the Malabar Coast with great inland cities such as the temple city of Madurai, with branches to all the major mercantile centers.

The network of caravan routes was established before the great Indian Mauryan Empire (from about 325 BC), with the Mauryans maintaining the routes for the merchants. By this time, the essential Malabar spices were used throughout the subcontinent. In maritime trade, by the beginning of the first century BC, seamen traded in their Indian Ocean dhows south to Sri Lanka, east to Indonesia, Cambodia, and China, and possibly west to Babylon and Madagascar. Jewish and Arab merchants were well versed in the sea routes to the Malabar Coast at this point and prospered within the region. The fragrant 19th century spice "godowns" (warehouses) of Jew Town in Cochin remain to this day.

South India flourished greatly when, in the first century AD the Greek mariner Hippalus rediscovered the monsoon winds that had allowed the Ancient Egyptians to sail across the Indian Ocean more swiftly. The Romans cast aside fantastical tales of the dangerous cinnamon harvest concocted by the Arabs to keep competitors away, and set sail for Malabar. The romance of India beckoned—and even the Emperor Trajan, observing the ships setting off from the Red Sea, lamented that he was too old to undertake the journey to enjoy India's marvels. The Romans established trading stations not only on the southwestern Malabar Coast, but along the opposite Coromandel coast. Like Alexander before them and the colonial empires after, the Romans

continued a European quest for black pepper that would change the course of history. Pepper became so valuable that it was traded ounce for ounce with gold—and was eventually demanded by both Attila the Hun and the Goths as part of the ransom of Rome.

In the centuries after the fall of the Roman Empire, the great South Indian kingdoms, such as the enlightened Vijayanagara, prospered through trade in spices, gems, and textiles, while raids into Southeast Asia and southern China brought them riches.

The dawn of Europe's Age of Exploration coincided with the rise of the Mughal Empire, stretching over the northern Subcontinent. But, looming over the horizon, was the arrival of the Portuguese ...

Vasco da Gama's voyage around Africa's Cape of Good Hope proved monumental for Europe and positively destructive for the East. Ending the Venetian monopoly (page 36) in pepper and other spices, he arrived in Malabar in 1498 to meet the Zamorin of Calicut. Asked if he could take a pepper stalk to replant in Portugal, the Zamorin casually replied that da Gama could take Malabar's pepper but never its unique monsoon rains. Da Gama's initial request for spices was scuppered by

local Arab merchants and the wealthy ruler. But, to the horror of the Zamorin, the Portuguese came back like thunder, quickly taking control of the spice trade and capturing territories from Goa on the west coast to Ceylon (Sri Lanka) in the south. Ships transported their precious spice cargoes from Goa to Lisbon, feeding both cities' wealth and Europe's hunger for spices. Goa was christened *Goa Dourada* or *Roma do Oriente* for its splendor. In the midst of it all, the Portuguese also brought the chile to India, and it spread like wildfire.

Portuguese rule, however, was short-lived, as other colonial regimes proved winners in the spice race. Although the Dutch captured Ceylon and Malabar, by the 17th century they were concentrating mostly on Southeast Asia (page 118). While other European powers from the Danes to the French chartered their own East India Companies, Britain's East India Company dwarfed their successes. Blocked by the Dutch in the Spice Islands, it looked to Ceylon and India.

Crucially, after stalling for years, in 1619, the Mughal emperor Jahangir finally allowed the English to trade in the Gujarati port of Surat, thus giving them a foothold. By 1668, Bombay had become their main port and their

continued expansion led to British rule over India—the Raj. It created a trade monopoly beyond the island nation's wildest dreams.

Today, there is no doubt that independent India, Sri Lanka, Pakistan, and Bangladesh, along with the Himalayan kingdoms and Afghanistan, have all held fast to thousands of years of tradition, despite early foreign influences and later, colonial rule. Spicing is as varied across South Asia as it has ever been. And though not in the dhows or galleons of yesteryear, pepper, cinnamon, cardamom, and myriad spices from the region still find their way around the world, while more unusual spices like cubeb, long pepper, and zedoary are waiting to be rediscovered in the West.

Above, from left: Buckets of cardamom, the world's second most expensive spice after saffron • Cardamom garden in Kerala: the pods grow on pannicles that shoot out along the ground under the leaves • Pepper grows in tiny bunches, like grapes, on a creeper clinging to trees • Freshly picked green peppercorns; they must be brined immediately to prevent their reacting with oxygen and turning black • Fully ripe red-brown peppercorns are dried and husked to produce white peppercorns.

indian vegetarian fritters
bondas, pakoras, or wadas

½ large cucumber, cut crosswise into thick slices

½ large cauliflower, broken into florets

peanut or safflower oil, for deep-frying

Batter

2 cups chickpea flour (called gram flour or besan in Asian markets and farina de ceci in Italian gourmet stores)

½ teaspoon ajwain seeds (optional)*

½ teaspoon cumin seeds

a large pinch of chili powder

1 teaspoon sea salt

Green chutney

2 handfuls of mint leaves, chopped

1 handful of fresh cilantro, chopped

2 green chiles, chopped

freshly squeezed juice of ½ lemon

a pinch of salt

thick plain yogurt (not low-fat), (optional)

To serve

chutneys or Indian pickles

lemon wedges

Serves 4–6

See note on dough and batter, page 4

*Ajwain (lovage) seeds are used frequently in snacks like these, and are considered an excellent digestive. Sold in Indian or Pakistani stores, they have a slightly bitter, thyme-like flavor, and are often used in recipes which include chickpea flour.

Bondas, pakodas or pakoras, and wadas are all favorite street food in the Indian subcontinent. These deep-fried vegetable snacks go well with local chutneys (savory or sweet). Many Indian chutneys are made with fresh herbs, rather than the sweet chutneys with which most people in the West are familiar. I've given one example here, and you can also serve Indian pickles (you'll find an interesting selection in Indian stores).

To make the chutney, put the mint, cilantro, chiles, lemon juice, and salt into a blender and blend to a purée, adding water to let the blades run. Serve as is, or stir in the yogurt.

To make the batter, put the chickpea flour into a large bowl and add the spices and salt. Mix with a fork, breaking up any lumps. Add enough water (2–4 tablespoons at a time) to make a thick, smooth batter, beating to achieve the right consistency. The batter should be thick enough to coat and cling to the vegetables.

Heat the oil in a deep saucepan to 375°F or until a cube of bread turns brown in 30 seconds. Dip a cucumber slice into the batter and coat well. Using tongs, carefully slide it into the oil. Fry in batches without overcrowding the pan, for a few minutes until golden, turning them several times. As each piece is done, lift it out with a slotted spoon or tongs and drain in a colander lined with paper towels. As soon as one batch is drained, transfer the pieces to a platter and keep them warm in a low oven until all are cooked. When all the cucumber has been fried, repeat with the cauliflower, which will take slightly longer to cook.

Serve with lemon wedges and a chutney or Indian pickle.

Note These fritters can be made with all sorts of vegetables and the spices can be varied too. Southern bondas use curry leaves and spices such as asafoetida and mustard seeds, while Bombay bondas or batat wadas may call for ginger, turmeric, chiles, and garlic. Slices of eggplant, zucchini, green bell peppers, or sliced or mashed potatoes also make good bondas, but if using mashed potatoes, the spices are fried in oil and added to the mash rather than the batter.

2½ lb. pumpkin, peeled, seeded, and cut into medium chunks

½ teaspoon ground turmeric

2 tablespoons safflower oil or ghee (clarified butter)

½ cinnamon stick

4–5 cardamom pods, bruised

1 medium onion, finely chopped

1 inch fresh ginger, peeled and grated

2 garlic cloves, crushed

⅔ cup canned chopped tomatoes

2 teaspoons ground cumin

2 teaspoons ground coriander

½ teaspoon sugar or jaggery (palm sugar)

⅓ cup light cream

¼ teaspoon ground white cardamom (from seeds only, not pods), plus extra for dusting

sea salt and freshly ground black pepper

fresh cilantro, to serve

Serves 4

rato farshi nepali pumpkin

From my favorite Nepalese restaurant in Britain, the Gurkha Kitchen.

Put the pumpkin into a saucepan, cover with water, then add a pinch of salt and half the turmeric. Bring to a boil, reduce the heat, and cook for about 12 minutes or until tender. Drain, reserving ⅓ cup of the cooking liquid. Set aside. (You could also save the remaining liquid as a vegetable stock if you wish; freeze for later use.)

Heat the oil or ghee in a skillet, then add the cinnamon, cardamom pods, and remaining ¼ teaspoon turmeric. Sauté briefly until aromatic (take care not to burn). Add the onion and sauté for about 6 minutes. Remove the cardamom and cinnamon and add the ginger and garlic. Sauté for a few more minutes over low heat, until the onion is very soft.

Add the tomatoes, pumpkin liquid, cumin, and coriander. Mix well and cook until the tomatoes have boiled down into a thick sauce. Add the pumpkin and mash into the sauce until it is well blended. Continue to cook, stirring regularly, for 5–6 minutes until soft. Add the sugar or jaggery, the cream, and ground cardamom. Cook for a further 1 minute. Taste and adjust the seasoning, then serve hot, topped with cilantro.

2 tablespoons peanut or safflower oil or ghee

1 lb. paneer cheese (2 blocks), halved lengthwise (see note)

¼ teaspoon ground turmeric

¼–½ teaspoon chili powder

1 teaspoon cumin seeds

1 medium onion, finely chopped

14 oz. (3 cups) shelled peas, fresh or frozen

1–1½ teaspoons Punjabi Garam Masala (South Asian Spice Mixes, page 95)

sea salt

To serve (optional)

a handful of cilantro, chopped

2–3 red chiles, seeded and sliced

Indian breads

Serves 6

mattar paneer peas and cheese

In India, the cheese is usually homemade, so I give a recipe below.

Heat 1 tablespoon oil or ghee in a nonstick skillet and swirl to coat. When hot, add the paneer. Sear for about 4 minutes or until brown. Turn and brown the other side. Remove from the pan and, when cool enough to handle, cut into cubes.

Heat the remaining tablespoon oil or ghee in the skillet. Add the turmeric, chili powder, and cumin and sizzle briefly. Add the onion and sauté over low heat for 8 minutes or until soft. Add the peas, garam masala, and salt and stir-fry for a few minutes, until the peas are cooked. Add the paneer, mix, and warm through. Top with the cilantro and chiles, if using. Serve hot with pooris, parathas, or naan (Indian breads).

Note Paneer, sold in Indian stores, has a firm texture, ideal for sautéing and grilling. To make your own, put 2 tablespoons lemon juice into a bowl with 4 cups milk. When set, drain the curd through cheesecloth. Weigh it down with a plate on top to make it firmer.

dill baath
south indian spiced rice with dill

1³/₄ cups basmati rice

¹/₃ cup safflower oil

¹/₄ cup Baath Masala
(South Asian Spice Mixes, page 105)

Tarka and dill

3 tablespoons safflower oil or ghee*

1 tablespoon black mustard seeds

1 teaspoon channa dhaal (yellow lentils)

1 teaspoon urid dhaal (white lentils)

1 teaspoon cumin seeds

³/₄ teaspoon asafoetida (hing)**

¹/₂ teaspoon ground turmeric

4 oz. fresh dill, central and any tough
stems discarded, fronds chopped

3 tablespoons Baath Masala

sea salt

Serves 4–6

*The choice of oil varies according to the
dish, the community or the region.
Maharashtrans often use peanut oil, in
Kerala, cooks rely on coconut oil, and
Bengalis like mustard oil, especially for fish.
Karnatakans like safflower oil or ghee.*

**Asafoetida is an important Indian spice and
enhances the flavor of other spices. It is
used instead of garlic and onions by some
religious communities, especially Brahmins.
It is at the heart of Karnatakan Brahmin
vegetarian cooking, of which this dish is a
delicious example.*

Some people are surprised that dill is used in Indian recipes, but it is relished by various communities. This South Indian recipe, *sohpseegay sohp baath* in my language, hails from Karnataka. In South India, where rice is king, such a spiced rice dish accompanies plain white rice and other dishes. It can also be eaten on its own. Make the baath masala ahead of time. You can use this for other South Indian baath (spiced rice dishes), adding vegetables like green sweet peppers instead of the dill, or a mixture of vegetables like carrots, peas, and string beans. The spicing is quite distinctive, combining a highly fragrant toasted and ground mixture with typically Southern whole spices fried in oil (the tarka).

Put the rice into a wide, heavy saucepan with a tight-fitting lid. Add 3³/₄ cups water and bring to a boil. Reduce the heat to the lowest setting. Line the inside of the lid with a dish towel and cover tightly so that no steam escapes. (This step is very important—gather the edges of the towel and fold over the top of the lid to keep the towel from coming into contact with the flame.) Gently simmer for 15 minutes, then turn off the heat completely and let steam, still tightly covered, for a further 10 minutes.

To make the tarka, put the oil or ghee into a small saucepan and heat until hot. Add the mustard seeds, yellow and white lentils, cumin seeds, asafoetida, and turmeric all at once. Cover the pan, reduce the heat to medium and let the spices sizzle and pop. Remove the pan from the heat and add the chopped dill, baath masala, and salt. Stir over low heat until the dill is nicely wilted and the masala is well mixed—add a little water if necessary. Remove from the heat.

Transfer the freshly cooked rice to a large mixing bowl, fluff up with a fork, and sprinkle ¹/₃ cup oil over the top. Add ¹/₄ cup baath masala and mix well. Stir in the tarka dill mixture so the rice is nicely coated—use two wooden forks or your hands to make sure the herbs and masala coat all the rice. Serve warm with other dishes.

Note Do not be tempted to uncover the rice at any time during the cooking/steaming period. It should be left alone for perfect results.

konju masala
spiced coconut shrimp

2 garlic cloves, chopped

1 inch fresh ginger, peeled and chopped

2 tablespoons safflower, peanut, or coconut oil*

4 small tomatoes, peeled and chopped

2 teaspoons white vinegar (wine or malt)

1 lb. uncooked shelled jumbo shrimp

sea salt

freshly shaved coconut, to serve

Masala paste

1 small onion, quartered

grated flesh of 1/2 coconut, fresh or frozen

2 black peppercorns

2 red chiles, seeded

1/4 teaspoon ground turmeric

2 teaspoons ground coriander

1/2 teaspoon black mustard seeds

Tarka spice-fry

1 tablespoon safflower, peanut, or coconut oil*

a few curry leaves**

a few red chiles, seeded and sliced

Serves 4

*Edible grade coconut oil is sold in many Indian stores and is popular in Kerala, the "Land of Coconuts."

**Curry leaves are always best fresh, and are often available in Indian or Southeast Asian markets. Fresh ones may be frozen. If absolutely necessary, dried ones may be used instead. Please note that curry leaves are not related to the gray-leaved curry plant grown in some herb gardens.

A recipe from Kerala, the long and fertile state in India's southwest. Kerala's thus-far unspoilt Malabar Coast has for thousands of years been a magnet for merchants and nations in search of Eastern spices. The streets of the spice quarter of the beautiful old port city of Cochin are lined with "godowns," 19th-century spice warehouses, with delicious scents of ginger and cinnamon, pepper and cassia issuing from their cavernous doorways. Kerala, like most of South India, reveres the coconut, so this shrimp and coconut recipe is a good example of its fine seafood dishes. Rice and pooris (South Indian breads) are delicious served with this dish.

Put all the masala ingredients into a blender and work into a thick paste, adding a dash of water if necessary to let the blades run. Remove and set aside. Put the garlic and ginger into the clean blender and grind to a paste. Alternatively, use a mortar and pestle.

Heat the 2 tablespoons oil in a wok or skillet. Add the garlic and ginger paste and sauté for a few seconds. Add the masala paste and stir-fry until the paste leaves the sides of the pan, about 8–10 minutes. Add the chopped tomatoes, vinegar, salt, and 1 cup water. Bring to a boil, add the shrimp, reduce the heat, and cook for 2–3 minutes, until the shrimp turn pink. Transfer to a serving bowl.

To prepare the tarka, heat the oil in a small skillet, add the curry leaves and red chiles, and sauté for about 45 seconds or so (this is called "tempering").

Pour the tempered tarka over the shrimp, top with shaved coconut, and serve.

chettinad chicken

chicken with chettinad spice-fry

8 large dried red chiles

2 tablespoons coriander seeds, toasted in a dry skillet

1 medium onion, finely chopped

1 inch fresh ginger, peeled and grated

4 boneless, skinless chicken breasts, cut into chunks

3 tomatoes, chopped

2 teaspoons tamarind concentrate (or tamarind water, to taste, page 121)

sea salt

Tarka spice-fry

2 tablespoons peanut oil or ghee

1/4 teaspoon turmeric

4 black peppercorns

1/4 teaspoon fennel seeds

1/4 teaspoon cumin seeds

a few curry leaves (optional)*

To serve

a handful of cilantro, chopped (optional)

2–4 green chiles, halved and seeded (optional)

plain yogurt

serves 4

Curry leaves are available in Indian stores (see page 85).

A dish from the Chettiar community of Tamil Nadu in southeast India. The Chettiars have always been famed for their business acumen and great wealth. A number of their fine mansions remain in Madras (now Chennai), and the modern Chettiar community still sticks to its traditions. They have a penchant for fiery food—plenty of chiles combined with coriander seeds and, often, extra black pepper. Having grown up with this method, I can verify that the toasting of the coriander seeds is typically southern—and what an aroma! This is a simple, hot Chettinad chicken dish, with plenty of broth to pour over rice. Alternatively, the liquid can be cooked down to a thick coating for the chicken, another popular treatment. Take your pick.

Using a mortar and pestle, blender, or spice mill, grind the dried chiles and toasted coriander seeds to a fine powder. Set aside.

To make the tarka, put the oil or ghee into a skillet and heat well. Add the turmeric, peppercorns, fennel and cumin seeds, and curry leaves, if using. Let sizzle briefly, then add the onion. Sauté for a few minutes, then add the ginger. Sauté for a further 6 minutes or so, until the onion is soft. If necessary, add a dash of water to prevent the mixture sticking to the pan.

Add the chicken and toss well to coat with the tarka. Sauté until the chicken begins to brown. Add enough water to cover, about 1 1/3 cups, then the tomatoes. Bring to a boil, reduce the heat, and simmer gently until the chicken is cooked, about 8–10 minutes. A few minutes before the end of cooking time, stir in 1 1/4 tablespoons of the reserved ground chile-coriander spice blend (or more, to taste). Put the tamarind concentrate into a bowl, add a ladle of liquid, stir to dissolve, then stir into the pan.* Sprinkle with the cilantro, top with the chiles, then serve with yogurt.

*Variation If you would like a thicker sauce, at this point transfer the pieces of chicken to a plate and keep them warm. Bring the liquid to a boil and simmer until reduced and thickened. Return the chicken to the pan, turn to coat, reheat, then serve.

spicy lamb in almond milk
badami elachi gosht

2 tablespoons unsalted butter or ghee
(clarified butter)

5 green cardamom pods, bruised

½ cinnamon stick

2½ lb. leg of lamb, well trimmed, boned,
and cut into chunks, or 1¾ lb. boned

⅓ cup plain yogurt, beaten

¼ teaspoon cardamom seeds (not pods)

1½ cups heavy cream

sea salt

Wet paste

2 large garlic cloves, sliced

1½ large onions, quartered

4 green chiles, seeded and
coarsely chopped

⅓ cup ground almonds, or ½ cup slivered
almonds, ground to a meal in a blender

To serve

freshly ground white pepper

finely sliced red onion, soaked in
a little vinegar

unroasted slivered almonds

boiled basmati rice

naan bread

light Indian vegetables side dishes, such as
those on page 80

Serves 4–6

Rich and creamy and steeped in plenty of almond and cardamom sauce, this "white" dish is a refined affair, like many a Moghul recipe developed for kings and courtiers. The wet paste of garlic, chiles, almonds, and onions provides body and a typically northern flavor (although this combination is popular in other parts of India too), while the cardamom and cinnamon scent the butter or ghee before other ingredients are added. White pepper is classically used in this dish, in keeping with its color.

To make the wet paste, put the garlic, onions, chiles, and almonds into a blender and blend until smooth, adding a little water to let the blades run. Alternatively, use a mortar and pestle. Set aside.

Melt the butter or ghee in a large, heavy saucepan and add the cardamom pods and cinnamon stick. Let the spices flavor the butter for 1–2 minutes, then add the wet paste. Sauté the paste for 8 minutes until thickened, stirring frequently to avoid burning.

Add the lamb and stir-fry until brown. Then add the yogurt and enough water to cover, about 1–1½ cups. Beat well. Heat until almost boiling, stirring constantly. Partly cover with a lid, reduce the heat to low, and simmer very gently for 45 minutes. (Lamb cooked over low heat becomes very tender.)

Remove the lid, then stir in the cardamom seeds and salt. Cook for 30 minutes longer. (The sauce may look slightly separated, but don't worry.)

Finally, stir in the cream, increase the heat, and bring to a boil. Reduce the heat and simmer gently for a few minutes to let the sauce thicken slightly. Stir in the cinnamon, if using. Sprinkle with white pepper, sliced red onion, and a few slivered almonds. Serve with boiled rice or a pulow (page 69), naan bread, and light Indian vegetable side dishes, such as those on page 80.

afghan boulanee

1 cup plus 2 tablespoons bread flour, plus extra for dusting

1⅓ cups whole-wheat flour

1 teaspoon sea salt

1 tablespoon peanut or safflower oil, plus extra for sealing and deep-frying

Chai Masala (South Asian Spice Mixes page 97), to serve

Vegetable filling

3 medium potatoes

1 teaspoon sea salt

6 scallions, chopped

2 tablespoons safflower oil

2 teaspoons cumin seeds

Serves 10 (makes 20)

See note on doughs and batters, page 4.

Stuffed fried pastries like this are found throughout the Middle East and South Asia, with various names like sambosek, borek, and samosa. Afghanistan's boulanee are usually made with leeks or potatoes, and sometimes both. In Afghanistan, spices still arrive from South Asia via animal caravan trade routes. According to Mike Edwards of *National Geographic*, Afghanistan's "Wakhan route ... served for perhaps 2000 years as a highway of trade and cultural exchange" while "lush pasture in the foothills of the Pamir mountains in northern Afghanistan served as a campsite for generations of travelers on the trade route to China." · Afghans themselves use spices with a light hand.

To make the filling, cook the potatoes in boiling salted water until tender, then drain and return to the saucepan. Add the salt and mash well. Stir in the scallions with a wooden spoon. Heat the oil in a small saucepan and add the cumin. Sauté for 30 seconds and pour over the potatoes. Stir a spoonful of mashed potatoes into the small saucepan to sponge up all the spiced oil, then stir back into the large saucepan. Cover and set aside.

To make the dough, put both flours and salt into a large bowl. Add 1 tablespoon oil and about ¾ cup water, or enough to make a stiff, pliable dough. Knead well for at least 10 minutes. Cover with a damp dish towel and let rest for 20–30 minutes.

Transfer to a work surface and divide into 20 small balls, about the size of a walnut. Cover them with the dish towel. Dust a work surface with flour, and roll out one of the balls to about 5 inches diameter, dusting with flour as necessary to stop it sticking. The dough should be very thin so the boulanee will be light. Put about 2 heaped tablespoons of the vegetable filling on one side of the round and spread it out with a spoon. Brush the edges of the dough with a little oil, and fold in half to form a crescent. Press the edges together, then fold them over on each other. Press with the tines of a fork to seal. Put onto a plate or tray and cover with a cloth. Repeat until all the boulanee are made (don't let them touch, or they will stick together).

Heat the oil in a deep saucepan to 375°F or until a cube of bread will brown in 30 seconds. Fry the boulanee one at a time on both sides until golden brown. Remove with a mesh strainer, then drain in a colander lined with paper towels. Repeat until all are made, removing them from the colander in batches and setting out on a serving tray, so they won't soak up any more oil. Keep them warm in a low oven until all are cooked.

Serve hot, either plain or with a dip or chutney, and cups of Chai Masala (page 97)

creamy saffron dessert
seviyan kheer/shavagay payasa

4 tablespoons unsalted butter

¼ cup raw unsalted cashews*

1½ tablespoons raisins

3 oz. Indian wheat vermicelli, broken into 1-inch lengths**

3 cups whole milk

½ cup minus 1 tablespoon sugar

½ teaspoon ground cardamom, preferably white (ground seeds, not pods) or the seeds from 1–2 cardamom pods

a large pinch of saffron threads

Topping

2 tablespoons unsalted butter

1 tablespoon raisins

1 tablespoon raw unsalted cashews

1 tablespoon shelled unsalted pistachios

a few saffron strands soaked in 1 tablespoon warm milk

a pinch of ground cardamom

Serves 4–6

*Cashews are produced in South India and Goa. In the North, this might be made with pistachios, almonds, or charoli nuts (a little like pine nuts), or a combination.

**Available from Indian/Pakistanis stores. Alternatively, use regular vermicelli pasta.

This scented vermicelli milk dessert is imbued with all the fragrance of saffron and cardamom (other versions include rosewater). It is a favorite all over India, known as payasa or payasam in the South and kheer in the North. Spices vary only slightly, but can make all the difference in flavor.

Melt the butter in a heavy saucepan. Add the cashews and raisins and sauté until the cashews are golden and the raisins plump. Add the broken vermicelli and sauté briefly in the butter, until it wilts and is evenly golden. (It will feel as if you are sautéing straw at this stage, but the vermicelli softens quickly.)

Add 2 cups of the milk and bring to a boil over medium-high heat, being careful not to let it burn. As soon as the milk reaches boiling point, lower the heat and add the sugar, cardamom, and saffron and stir. Cook for a few minutes until the mixture thickens and the vermicelli is cooked through. The mixture will be quite thick at this stage—since I like my payasa with a little more "flow," I add the remaining milk at this point. Stir well and remove from the heat, but keep hot.

To prepare the topping, heat the butter in a small saucepan, add the raisins, cashews, and pistachios and stir-fry for a few minutes until golden (don't let the butter burn).

Stir the mixture again and spoon into small bowls. Sprinkle with the soaked saffron, ground cardamom, and buttered cashews, pistachios, and raisins and serve hot, though it is also delicious when cold.

Variations You could also make this dessert with just one of the spices listed, or with saffron and rosewater. If you use commercially made rosewater, it will usually contain citric acid, so you must wait until the mixture cools completely before adding it, or the milk will curdle. When ready to serve, top with a few unsprayed rose petals.

south asian spice mixes

The people of the Indian Subcontinent could not survive without their multifarious spice mixtures. Each region has its own blends, as does each community. There are different blends for different kinds of foods, and blends that are unique to each family, handed down from mother to daughter. A typical mortar is often round or rectangular, and the pestle is like a short, thick, stone rolling pin.

Tarka Spice-Fry

The tarka is the backbone of Indian spicing. It is essentially a method of releasing the flavor of spices, by sautéing them in hot fat (oil or ghee). As a rule, heat a small amount of oil or ghee first, before adding the spices. Sauté briefly as spices burn easily. The tarka can be mixed through a dish, as in raita (yogurt dip) or dhaal (lentil sauce), or used at the beginning of a dish, before other ingredients are added and cooked. Although I've labeled the tarkas, there are many combinations of spices that can be used, and different communities within regions have their own combinations, many with turmeric. Here are a few of the most widely used tarkas.

Simple tarka Ground turmeric, chili powder, and cumin seeds.

Raita tarka Use the simple tarka, or a mixture of fennel seeds and turmeric.

Pulow tarka Cinnamon stick, whole cloves, cardamom pods, whole peppercorns, bay leaves, and, if you want a yellow pulow, add turmeric too.

North Indian/Pakistani tarkas Black cardamom pods, cinnamon stick, and black cumin seeds; or black cardamom pods, whole cloves, and cinnamon stick; or green cardamom pods, cumin seeds, and cloves.

Punjabi tarka Nigella seeds, turmeric, fenugreek seeds, and chili powder.

Bengali/Bangladeshi tarkas Use the Panch Phoran mixture opposite.

South Indian/Sri Lankan tarkas Curry leaves, mustard seeds, asafoetida, ground turmeric, and chili powder or chiles, with or without the addition of a few channa (yellow) or urid (white) lentils, depending on the dish; or cumin and mustard seeds, turmeric, and green chiles; or red chiles, fenugreek, and mustard seeds.

Western tarka White or black cumin seeds, mustard seeds, turmeric, and chili powder.

Ginger, Garlic, and Chile Paste

This wet paste is used in many dishes. Sometimes onions are blended with the other ingredients, or they may be added in chopped form, or sometimes not at all. Often, ginger and chiles are pounded together on their own; especially by some religious communities that eschew garlic.

1 inch fresh ginger, peeled and chopped

2 green chiles, chopped

2 garlic cloves, chopped

Using a mortar and pestle or small blender, grind the ingredients together, adding a dash of water or oil if necessary. (Don't add too much water—the paste should be thick.) Use fresh, or make it a day in advance and refrigerate.

Garam Masala

Garam means "hot," *masala* means "spice"—this spice blend, originally from northern India, is now widely used throughout the country. The combination of whole spices varies from region to region and household to household. Most do not require the spices to be dry-roasted first, although some households do dry-roast. The standard versions use easy-to-find spices, but do try the others too, as the subtle differences enhance individual dishes. Please do make your own, as most commercial blends are disappointing.

Punjabi

2 tablespoons cumin seeds

2 teaspoons black cumin seeds

seeds from 2 green cardamom pods

2 black cardamom pods

2-inch piece of cinnamon stick

5 whole cloves

2 bay leaves

Using a mortar and pestle, mini-blender, or spice grinder, grind all the spices to a fine powder. Store in an airtight jar.

Standard North Indian Grind black peppercorns, cinnamon, cloves, and cumin together. A variation is to add whole green cardamom pods and coriander seeds.

Pakistani Add fennel and coriander seeds to the Punjabi mixture.

Kashmiri Similar to Pakistani, but without the green cardamom and with mace and sometimes saffron added. Saffron is grown in Kashmir.

Baath Masala

A highly fragrant mixture for South Indian spiced rice with vegetables or herbs. When buying the lentils, make sure you ask for channa and urid split lentils, not whole lentils. My Mom still makes the finest baath masala—this is her recipe.

¼ cup channa dhaal (yellow lentils)

½ cup urid dhaal (white lentils)

7 medium dried red chiles (not Thai bird's eye)

9 whole cloves

1 cardamom pod

2 cinnamon sticks, broken into small pieces

¼ cup unsweetened shredded coconut

4 tablespoons coriander seeds

Put the channa dhaal into a skillet and dry-roast over medium heat for 30 seconds or so, stirring all the time. Add the urid dhaal, dried red chiles, cloves, cardamom pod, broken cinnamon sticks, shredded coconut, and coriander seeds. Dry-roast, stirring constantly, until you can smell a toasted aroma and steam begins rising from the pan. The lentils in particular should be roasted nicely.

Transfer to a mortar and pestle, mini-blender, or spice grinder (coffee grinder kept just for spices). Grind coarsely and set aside until ready for use.

Panch Phoran

Also known as podni, this famous East Indian mixture of whole spices is from Bengal and Bangladesh, but it is also enjoyed elsewhere in the east and north. It is a mixture of five spices (*panch* means "five")—equal quantities of the following whole spice seeds; cumin, fennel, fenugreek, black mustard, and nigella (also known as kalonji or black onion seeds). Heat a small amount of oil or ghee in a skillet, add the spices, and sauté briefly to develop the aromas. Take care, because they burn easily.

Char Masala

An Afghan four-spice (*char* means "four") blend used like garam masala. The spices vary and they are ground together into a powder. Combinations could include black or green cardamom, whole cloves, cinnamon stick, and cumin.

Sarina or Rasam Pudi

Pudi means "powder," and this is a quintessentially South Indian spice blend—complex and utterly satisfying when used to make the dhaal, tomato, and tamarind soup known as saru (always accompanied by rice) or the thin, dhaal-less version to drink, called rasam. *Rasa* means "liquid or essence" and this is very much the essence of South India. Again, the recipe varies from house to house—this comes from my Aunt Manjula.

3 teaspoons safflower oil

½ teaspoon asafoetida (hing)

1 tablespoon black peppercorns

1 tablespoon cumin seeds

1 tablespoon black mustard seeds

1 tablespoon fenugreek seeds (methi)

½ cup coriander seeds

5 fresh curry leaves

¼ teaspoon ground turmeric

1 oz. large dried red chiles

Heat 1 teaspoon of the oil in a skillet, add the asafoetida and black pepper, and toast, stirring with a wooden spoon. Remove the spices to a plate and set aside.

In the same skillet, toast the cumin, then the mustard seeds, then the fenugreek, as the cooking time and temperature for each one varies.

Heat another 1 teaspoon oil in the skillet and fry the coriander seeds and curry leaves. Remove to a plate and add the turmeric.

With the final teaspoon of oil, sauté the red chiles. Grind all the ingredients to a fine powder and store in an airtight jar. (You can refrigerate the pudi if you'd like to store it for a longer time.)

Tamarind Gojju

This is another of Mom's sublime recipes—a gojju is the sweet, sour, and spicy jam-like condiment used for the famous tamarind rice of Karnataka and Tamil Nadu. For tamarind rice, simply add a dash of oil and few tablespoons of this mixture to hot, cooked long-grain rice and let it melt. Mix gently but well (the colour should be a brick red). Gojju is also served as a dip with other southern rice dishes; you could also use it as a chutney-like condiment or stir it into yogurt to make a delicious dip. This recipe is for a small quantity: you can always double or triple the recipe and store in the refrigerator if you want to use it regularly.

1 oz. lump tamarind (with seeds and fiber)

2 tablespoons jaggery (palm sugar) or sugar

about 1 teaspoon sarina/rasam pudi (left)

3 tablespoons safflower oil

¼ cup raw shelled peanuts

¼ teaspoon asafoetida (hing)

½ teaspoon channa dhaal (yellow lentils)

½ teaspoon urid dhaal (white lentils)

½ teaspoon ground turmeric

1 teaspoon mustard seeds

6 fresh curry leaves

sea salt

Put the tamarind into a bowl, add ⅔ cup hot water and soak for about 10–15 minutes. Squeeze the tamarind through your fingers in the water and continue until it has been squeezed into a pulp. Either remove all the tamarind bits with your fingers leaving only the paste behind (as most Indians do), or press through a strainer into a saucepan, making sure you squeeze out all the liquid. Discard the bits. Add the jaggery and blend in with a fork, pressing out any lumps. Cook the mixture over low heat, stirring regularly until it thickens. As it is thickening, add the sarina/rasam pudi and salt. Mix well and taste for heat—it should be sweet, sour, and fiery. Remove from the heat and set aside.

Heat the oil in a saucepan and add the peanuts. Stir-fry until toasted (take care not to burn). Reduce the heat and add the asafoetida, lentils, turmeric, mustard seeds, and curry leaves and cover with a lid. As soon as they sizzle, remove from the heat. Stir in the tamarind.

Chai Masala

Chai means "tea" and it is taken on its own, with snacks—and constantly! Always served with milk and sugar, it is a much-loved elixir. Chai Masala is tea infused with spices. If you want to be truly Indian in your endeavors, froth the chai as the chaiwallahs do, pouring the hot liquid from a great height from one

steel *lota* (tumbler) to another. This is why the drink is sometimes called "long tea," because of the great length of the tea as it is frothed. I'm sure this was the precursor to modern café latte or even cappuccino.

1 cinnamon stick, halved

4 whole cloves

6 cardamom pods

2 blades of mace

2 cassia buds, long pepper, or black peppercorns

a pinch of freshly grated nutmeg

a pinch of ground ginger

4–5 teaspoons Assam or Nilgiri tea leaves

1 cup milk

sugar or honey, to taste

Put the spices and 4 cups water into a saucepan and bring to a boil. Reduce the heat, cover, and simmer gently for 5 minutes. Add the tea leaves and brew for 1 minute before adding the milk. Stir and continue to brew to required strength (4 more minutes is perfect). Strain and serve with sugar or honey to taste, or froth from pan to pan or, if you have the knack, from tumbler to tumbler!

Variations Try cardamom on its own or with saffron; cinnamon; grated fresh ginger with honey, or other spices.

east asia

Although China, Japan, and Korea are old and venerable lands linked to the ancient spice trade by both land and sea, the region's use of spices is surprisingly understated compared with other Asian countries. None of the complex pastes or blends like those of, say, Malaysia or India have dented the regional cuisines. However some spice mixtures do regularly appear in the kitchen—Chinese five-spice powder, which correlates with the belief in "five flavors to live" (Chinese food and medicine have been closely linked for thousands of years), the seven-spice Japanese blend of sichimi togarashi, and Korea's complex, fermented chile paste, which takes months to prepare.

Some spices are important throughout East Asia. Ginger is foremost, with sesame not far behind. Strangely, although loved in all three countries, neither ginger nor sesame is native to the region. Ginger originated in tropical Asia but was long ago naturalized in China, its use promoted by Confucius in the fifth century BC. Black and white sesame seeds and sesame oil, brought from the Mediterranean some 2000 years ago, also found a welcome in here.

Chinese cassia, exquisitely shaped star anise, dried tangerine peel, numbing Szechuan pepper and its Japanese counterpart sansho, and potent green wasabi are all native spices. Others, such as cloves and black pepper, were traded along the Silk Road and sea lanes, and occasionally appear in the Chinese spice box, while in Korea the Portuguese-introduced American chile is indisputably king.

spices, silks and seclusion

The fabled Silk Road, the ancient overland trade route from Europe to China, was not one road, but a meandering network of caravan trails with dozens of branches. These branches linked the great cities and civilizations of the ancient and medieval world with the markets of East and West. The Indus Valley Harappa civilization, the cities of the Gangetic Plain, the Kingdoms of the Deccan peninsula, the Temple Cities of Angkor Wat, and the treasures of the Spice Islands all had to be linked with the Silk Road at some point to send their wares to the markets in Europe, and to receive commodities in return.

Although the success of the route is mostly attributed to China's Han emperors from around 200 BC, the route itself was used much earlier, probably from 600 BC. When the Hans rose to power, they fought off nomadic tribes (hence the Great Wall) and secured the Silk Road for travelers, opening it up for vigorous trade with the West.

Chinese silk was an expensive trophy in ancient times, prized especially by the Romans. They would travel to the ends of the earth to acquire silk, along with porcelain and spices. Ginger from Southeast Asia was one of the earliest spices to be traded along the route and greatly appreciated by both East and West. Likewise, the early Chinese loved black peppercorns and particularly long pepper from India to add to meat dishes.

From the West, via the Silk Road and sea traders, China received not only sesame and ginger—now such a feature of East Asian cuisines—but also caraway, coriander, and mustard. Other spices which now seem unusual for China were in evidence during the Tang period (618–c.906 AD), spices such as saffron from Persia and India, and possibly sumac from the Mediterranean. Even Indian green cardamom had been naturalized in southern China by this time.

There were various meeting points along the Silk Road, which stretched 3750 miles from Changan and the Indus to Antioch and Alexandria. Caravans passed on goods to other travelers and crafty middlemen. Hence spices and incense, feathers, animals, ivory, glass, gems, gold, and even religion would be transported back and forth, with merchants exchanging their wares and beliefs along the way. However, with the fall of the Han Dynasty in the third century AD, the Silk Road fell into disuse.

When the Mongols under Genghis Khan conquered Asia, they reopened the ancient Silk Road for just a century (1250–1350), with the Venetians making full use of its advantages. Marco Polo traveled along much of its distance on his way to his adventures in the court of Kublai Khan in China. He marveled at Chinese ports and was taken with the beauty of Hangzhou. Busy harbors saw merchants from far and wide, spices came from all directions and all ethnic groups converged. Polo wrote of thousands of baskets of pepper being loaded onto Chinese ships in Java. His itinerant Berber contemporary, Ibn Battuta, also witnessed the massive Chinese trading junks and their support boats, equipped for the many merchant families on board, sailing to Indian Ocean ports in search of spices and textiles. Vegetables and ginger were grown on board the junks—ginger as a preventative for scurvy as well as a valuable spice.

Just a century later, with the Mongols deposed, China looked outward for a rare period, as it sent its great admiral Zheng He—the "Three-Jeweled Eunuch"—on expeditions that took him all the way to East Africa, to Mogadishu, Malindi, and the great spice port of Zanzibar. Spurred on to buy pepper, the Chinese junks sailed from the Yangtze to India, then to Ceylon, Sumatra, Java, Siam, and, above all, Malacca.

Zheng He managed seven expeditions, one of which covered

36 states. The expeditions brought tributes in native spices and goods, but this period of friendly exploration was brought to a sudden halt after his last voyage, when all maritime trade was halted. From this time, the Chinese were prevented from traveling abroad or trading with foreigners, and China once again retreated into itself.

Historically, the use of mostly local spices (especially in Japan) can be attributed to this age-old East Asian distrust of foreign influences. Although China, Korea, and Japan had long traded with each other, and China in particular on and off with the rest of the world, the region has had a recurring tradition of suspicion towards foreign influence and foreign values.

In Japan, Portuguese traders first arrived near Kyushu in the 1500s, followed by missionaries. At first the Shogun was receptive, also encouraging trade with the Dutch and English. But, fearful of Christianity's influence, he expelled most of the foreigners and adopted a policy of seclusion that was maintained for the next 200 years. The Portuguese remained briefly, but from 1641 only Dutch VOC bachelors were allowed to conduct limited trade and only from Dejima in Nagasaki harbor. Hence, Japan's own unique cuisine developed without hindrance, with very few non-native spices. The Portuguese-introduced chile, for instance, appears rarely and then mostly in foreign dishes.

Korea, sandwiched between two mighty imperial powers, could not help but be influenced by the food and customs of both. It, too, cut itself off from foreign influences, but could not sustain the isolation for very long. Despite its suspicion of the West, Korea accepted both Christianity and the chile much more readily than either Japan or China, although chile use in China varies according to region. Even Korea's own spicy version of sushi, *kimbap*, is enjoyed with a fiery chile sauce as opposed to the wasabi beloved of the Japanese.

Neither Japan nor China could keep out the Western powers forever. After Vasco da Gama discovered the sea route around the Cape at the end of the 15th century, the monopoly of Venice (page 36) was broken and it was just a matter of time. European maritime might was too great and their desire for Oriental luxuries even greater. Japanese isolation ended with the arrival of the US East India Company in 1853.

In China, the Manchu emperor famously dismissed the first British envoy who came seeking trade relations by declaring, "There is nothing we lack … We have never set much store on strange … objects, nor do we need any more of your country's manufactures."

However, after the Opium Wars, China had been forced to open its gates. The British sailed up the Yangtze River to Nanking, where an eponymous treaty meant that the ports of Shanghai, Canton, Foochow, Ningpo, and Amoy were open for trade. France and the United States followed hot on their heels. Shanghai, which had been an important local trading port for centuries, now burgeoned into a vital international trading center. Only after the rise of the People's Republic of China did foreign traders move into Hong Kong, the vibrant Asian tiger admired throughout the world today.

From above left: Even today, camel caravans carry goods along the remnants of the Silk Road • Hong Kong took over as the major trading port of East Asia after the rise of the People's Republic of China • Usually available in powder or paste form, fresh wasabi root, on sale here in Kyoto's Nishiki-koji market, is a highly prized, luxury item.

pa jon korean pancakes
with white radish kimchi

2 cups buckwheat flour

1 cup rice flour

$\frac{1}{2}$ teaspoon salt

a pinch of sugar

1 teaspoon baking powder

1 small carrot, sliced into matchstick strips

2 oz. Chinese chives or regular chives, chopped ($\frac{3}{4}$ cup)

5 long green chiles, seeded and finely sliced into thin slivers

7 red bird's eye chiles, seeded and finely sliced into thin slivers

peanut oil, for sautéing

White radish kimchi

1 teaspoon sugar

2 tablespoons rice vinegar

1 large garlic clove, crushed

a pinch of sea salt

8 oz. daikon (white radish), peeled and grated (1$\frac{1}{4}$ cups)

Chile sesame dip

$\frac{1}{4}$ cup tamari or soy sauce

2$\frac{1}{2}$ tablespoons toasted sesame oil

1 garlic clove, crushed

1 teaspoon white sesame seeds, toasted in a dry skillet

$\frac{1}{2}$ teaspoon black sesame seeds, toasted in a dry skillet (optional)

1 red bird's eye chile, seeded and chopped (optional)

1 preserving jar (1 cup), sterilized (page 4)

Serves 4 (makes 8–10 pancakes)

In Korea, both fresh and dried chiles are used with great abandon. Sesame seeds, black and white, as well as sesame oil and the leaves of the wild sesame plant are also widely used. Kimchi is most familiar as a garlicky cabbage pickle, but there are actually hundreds of vegetable kimchis. This is an easy white radish version. Finally, the trick to this dish is a balanced ensemble—simple chile-laced pancakes, garlicky and sour kimchi, and salty hot dip. They must be served together, or the dish will lose the desired effect.

Make the kimchi 1–3 days before using. Put the sugar, vinegar, garlic, and salt into a bowl. Put the grated radish into a dish towel and squeeze well to remove excess water. Add the radish to the bowl and mix until well coated. While the jar is still hot, pour the kimchi into the jar and seal tightly. Let cool, then refrigerate until ready to use.

To make the dip, put the tamari and sesame oil into a bowl and beat well. Stir in the remaining ingredients and serve in 4 small dishes.

To make the pancakes, put the flours, salt, and sugar into a bowl and mix. Add the baking powder and gradually beat in enough water to make a smooth batter, the consistency of thin cream. Stir in the carrot and chives.

Heat about 1 tablespoon peanut oil in an 8-inch nonstick skillet. Add a few strips of green and red chiles, then a small ladle of batter, about $\frac{1}{2}$ cup. Swirl it over the base of the pan and cook over medium-low heat for 2 minutes on one side or until the bubbles turn into holes. Turn it over and cook for 1–2 minutes or until done (to test, pierce the middle with a fork—if it comes out clean, the pancake is ready). Stack on a plate and keep them warm in a low oven while you cook the remaining pancakes.

Serve hot with a dish of dip and a spoonful of kimchi on each plate. (You may wish to double the kimchi recipe as it always proves so popular.)

Note Pa jon don't usually contain baking powder, but I depart from tradition because I like the effect of raised pancakes. They can also be made with wheat flour or a mixture of wheat and rice flours. Finally, the trick to this dish is a balanced ensemble—simple chile-laced pancakes, garlicky and sour kimchi, and salty hot dip. They must be served together, or the dish will lose the desired effect.

norimaki with ginger and wasabi

Sushi rice

1 1/2 cups Japanese sushi rice

1 large garlic clove, crushed

2 1/2 tablespoons Japanese rice vinegar

1 1/2 tablespoons sugar

Large vegetable norimaki

1 sheet toasted nori

1 teaspoon black sesame seeds

2 strips of seeded cucumber, 1/2 x 4 inches long, cut with a vegetable peeler or mandoline

2 strips of carrot, 1/2 x 4 inches long, cut with a vegetable peeler or mandoline

1 scallion, halved lengthwise

Small salmon and/or tuna norimaki

2 sheets toasted nori, halved crosswise

Wasabi Paste (East Asian Spice Mixes, page 115)

1/2 teaspoon black sesame seeds

4 oz. sushi-grade salmon or tuna (super fresh), or a mixture of both, cut into 8 thin strips, about 4 inches long

To serve

2 tablespoons Wasabi Paste (East Asian Spice Mixes, page 115)

several slices of Pickled Ginger (page 114)

Japanese soy sauce (shoyu or tamari)

a sushi rolling mat covered in plastic wrap

Makes 6 large, 12 small

Norimaki are a type of sushi, which, to many people, epitomizes Japanese food. The dainty morsels of seaweed, rice, and fish or vegetables, so elegantly prepared, really are works of art on a plate. Although spices don't play a major role in Japanese cuisine, there are some notable exceptions—pickled ginger and wasabi. Fresh ginger pickled in rice vinegar and sugar is a superior palate cleanser—pleasing and sharp at the same time. Equally, wasabi (known as Japanese horseradish) may look harmless enough, but it produces a fiery kick that travels right up through the sinuses—immeasurably satisfying, even if that sounds masochistic! Finally, black sesame seeds are an appropriate seasoning and dark counterpoint against the white rice.

To make the sushi rice, put the rice into a heavy saucepan or rice cooker with 1 3/4 cups boiling water. Return to a boil, reduce the heat, cover with a lid, and simmer for about 10 minutes. Turn off the heat and let stand, still covered, for 15–20 minutes. Transfer the rice to a bowl and sprinkle with the garlic, sugar, and vinegar. Mix gently with a wooden spoon—don't stir too much. Set aside until the rice is warm.

To make the large norimaki, put the nori sheet on the plastic-wrapped sushi mat. With slightly moistened fingers (not too wet or the rice will fall apart), press a layer of rice onto the sheet, leaving a 1/2-inch margin at the far end. Sprinkle all over with the sesame seeds. Starting at the edge closest to you, and leaving a tiny margin, put a single line of cucumber strips across the rice, then a line of carrot strips close to the cucumber, then a line of scallion strips.

Starting at the near edge, carefully roll the mat, keeping the vegetables in place, to form a cylinder. Lift the mat away from the nori and press and roll the cylinder so it sticks together. (You may also rub a little rice vinegar at the edge of the nori to help it stick.) Transfer the cylinder to a chopping board. Using a sharp knife dipped in water, slice the cylinder in half, then each half into 3, giving 6 equal pieces. Transfer to a large serving platter.

Make small salmon and/or tuna norimaki in the same way, using 1/2 sheet of nori each. Add the rice in the same way, dot a little wasabi in a line across the rice, and sprinkle the sesame seeds on top. Put a line of salmon or tuna strips on top of the wasabi. Roll as above, but keep the fish in the center of the nori sheet. Repeat to make a second roll. Slice and add to the serving platter. Serve the sushi with a little wasabi paste, a few slices of pickled ginger, and tiny dishes of shoyu or tamari.

miso and wakame soup
with japanese seven-spice

2 tablespoons dried wakame seaweed

3 tablespoons miso paste

4 oz. firm tofu, cut into ½-inch cubes

1 scallion, trimmed and finely sliced

Shichimi Togarashi (East Asian Spice Mixes, page 115) or ground sansho pepper, to serve

Dashi*

1 piece dried kombu seaweed, 2 inches square

6 tablespoons dried bonito flakes (*ana-katsuo*)

Serves 4

*Instant dashi powder is widely available in larger supermarkets and Japanese stores. Labeled "dashi-no-moto," it is freeze-dried and very convenient. Use 1–2 teaspoons for this recipe.

Classic in its simplicity, miso soup warms and entices at the beginning of a Japanese meal. Sansho or mountain pepper is the Japanese cousin of Szechuan peppercorns, but more subtle. Neither is a peppercorn at all, but the seed pod of the prickly ash tree and, as well as the pods, the young shoots, flowers, and bitter berries are also used in cooking. Shichimi togarashi, the Japanese seven-spice blend, has sansho as one of its constituents. The Japanese ingredients in this soup are quite widely available—larger supermarkets, natural food and organic stores, and Asian markets will have many of them. They can be used in other recipes, so keep a stock in your pantry. The soup is definitely worth making—serve it as the Japanese do, in beautiful lacquer bowls.

To make the dashi, put the kombu into a large saucepan and add 2½ cups water. Bring to a boil and immediately remove the kombu (don't let it boil or it will become bitter).

Add the bonito flakes to a boiling water, simmer gently for 2–3 minutes, then remove from the heat. Let stand for a few minutes until the bonito settles to the bottom of the pan. Pour through a strainer lined with cheesecloth and reserve the liquid. (Alternatively, add 1–2 teaspoons instant dashi powder to boiling water and stir to dissolve.)

Meanwhile, soak the wakame in a large bowl of water for 10–15 minutes until fully opened. Drain and cut into small pieces.

Put the miso into a cup or bowl and mix with a few spoonfuls of dashi. Return the dashi to a low heat and add the diluted miso. Add the wakame and tofu to the pan and turn up the heat. Just before it reaches boiling point, add the finely chopped scallion and immediately remove from the heat. Do not boil.

Serve hot in individual soup bowls with a little shichimi togarashi or ground sansho pepper for sprinkling.

vegetable stir-fry
with szechuan peppercorns

1 teaspoon Szechuan peppercorns, plus extra to serve

2 tablespoons peanut oil

4 scallions, chopped

2 garlic cloves, sliced

1 small red bell pepper, seeded and finely sliced lengthwise

1 carrot, finely sliced lengthwise into matchstick strips

18 baby corn (candle corn), chopped into 3

freshly squeezed juice of 1/2 lemon

1/4 cup dark soy sauce or wheat-free tamari

1 small head of broccoli, broken into florets

14 sugar snap peas, trimmed

1 tablespoon toasted sesame oil

Serves 4

Szechuan peppercorns are an important spice in Chinese cookery, included in the well-known blend of Chinese five-spice. They are known by several names including Chinese pepper or flower pepper. Not related to black pepper, Szechuan peppercorns are unusual in appearance and taste. They are reddish berries, usually opened out, containing black shiny seeds which should be discarded. The berries smell fruity and woody at the same time with a peculiarly numbing bite, quite unlike regular pepper. More subdued Japanese sansho (see Miso and Wakame Soup, page 107) is closely related, while a larger, darker spice known as triffla or tirphal thrives in Maharashtra, India, and is probably another relation. Here, I've used Szechuan peppercorns in a simple stir-fry, where their effect can best be felt. They are readily available in Chinese stores. Serve this dish with noodles or rice and additional recipes such as the Red-Cooked Chicken in this chapter.

Discard any shiny black inner seeds from the peppercorns. Toast the peppercorns in a small skillet over low heat for 1–2 minutes until aromatic. Using a mortar and pestle, grind to a coarse powder.

Heat the peanut oil in a wok and add the scallions and garlic. Stir-fry over medium-high heat for 1 minute. Add the pepper, carrot, baby corn, lemon juice, and 1 tablespoon of the soy sauce and stir-fry for 2–3 minutes.

Add the broccoli, sugar snap peas, the ground Szechuan pepper, and the remaining soy sauce. Stir-fry briefly, cover, and cook for 4–5 minutes or until the vegetables are tender but still firm. Uncover and add the sesame oil. Stir and serve hot with a small dish of ground Szechuan pepper for guests to help themselves.

Note If you can't find Szechuan peppercorns, there is really no substitute. However, you can easily obtain a peppery bite with regular peppercorns. Try a mixture of pink, green, and black for a bit of variety, and add some freshly grated ginger to the stir-fry.

red-cooked chicken legs

2/3 cup dark soy sauce

3 tablespoons Chinese rice wine
or dry sherry

2 thin slices of fresh ginger

3 cinnamon sticks, halved

5 whole star anise

2 whole cloves

3 scallions

1/2 teaspoon grated orange or lemon zest

1 tablespoon fresh lemon juice

1/2 teaspoon sugar

4 large chicken legs (thighs and drumsticks)

Serves 4

Chinese red-cooking involves poaching meat, poultry, game, or even fish in a dark, soy-based sauce. When the sauce is spiced with star anise, cinnamon, and sometimes additional spices from the five-spice brigade, it is used as a "master sauce." You will sometimes find spices such as licorice root and citrus peel in a master sauce as well, depending on the dish. Master sauce is used like a stock, cooked first as in the recipe below, then stored for later use (I use the freezer). When it has been used a few times, it is considered mature and more desirable. Serve with rice or a noodle dish, stir-fried vegetables, and other Chinese dishes.

Pour the soy sauce and rice wine into a large saucepan and add 1 quart water. Add the ginger, cinnamon, star anise, cloves, scallions, orange or lemon zest, lemon juice, and sugar. Bring to a boil and turn off the heat. Set aside for at least 10 minutes to infuse the flavors.

Add the chicken legs and bring to a boil. Reduce the heat and simmer for 40 minutes, or until cooked through and tender.

Transfer the legs to a serving bowl or plate and spoon over some of the sauce. Alternatively, use a Chinese cleaver to chop them into bite-size pieces. Transfer any remaining sauce to an airtight container and refrigerate (or freeze) for later use.

Note When cooking "red" or master-sauce based recipes, it is important to get the right balance of liquids, or the sauce can be too strong. Regular soy sauce often contains wheat products: if you prefer wheat-free ingredients, use Japanese tamari soy sauce.

bulgogi

1 large boneless sirloin steak, 1–1 1/2 inches thick, about 1 lb., trimmed of fat

2 tablespoons tamari or other soy sauce

1 teaspoon toasted sesame oil

1–2 teaspoons sugar

1 garlic clove, crushed

1 inch fresh ginger, peeled and finely grated

2 scallions, trimmed and chopped

1–2 bird's eye chiles, red or green, seeded and chopped

a pinch of salt

To serve

lettuce leaves

kimchi (page 102)

a stove-top grill pan or skillet, lightly greased

Serves 4

Bulgogi is a Korean delight—as popular with tourists as it is with the locals. In restaurants the beef strips are grilled on table-top grills, but you could also cook them on aluminum foil over hot coals. Easiest of all, they can be seared in a very hot pan—the method used by most home cooks. Ginger and toasted sesame oil are included in the marinade, while chiles make their inevitable appearance, though the amount is up to you.

Bulgogi is an appetizer that can be made and served in two ways. Always sliced very thinly, the beef strips can be wide or narrow. The wide ones are served with rice and condiments, while the narrow ones are rolled up in lettuce leaves—an entirely satisfying way of eating this dish.

Freeze the steak for 1 hour so it will be easy to slice very thinly. Remove the steak from the freezer, then slice very thinly crosswise.

To make the marinade, put the tamari or soy, sesame oil, and sugar into a bowl and beat well. Stir in the garlic, ginger, scallions, chiles, and salt, then add the beef strips, mix well to coat, cover, and refrigerate for several hours to develop the flavors.

Heat a stove-top grill pan or skillet until very hot. Sear the strips of steak briefly on both sides until just done, working in batches so you don't overcrowd the pan. Either pile onto a large plate or on several smaller ones. Serve as a appetizer with lettuce and kimchi.

east asian spice mixes

Though not as numerous as the spice mixes of South and Southeast Asia, those of East Asia are subtle and exotic, including ginger, sesame, and spices such as dried tangerine peel, licorice root, and dried seaweed. Chinese spices are also linked to medicinal use.

Szechuan Seasoning

Easy to make, this spiced and toasted Chinese salt seasoning is used to sprinkle over foods.

1 teaspoon coarse salt

½ tablespoon Szechuan peppercorns

1 teaspoon Chinese five-spice powder

Put the salt and Szechuan peppercorns into a dry skillet and toast gently until both begin to brown (take care because they burn easily). Remove from the heat, let cool, grind to a powder, and mix in the five-spice powder.

Chinese Five-Spice Powder

This essential Chinese blend is made with a minimum of five spices—the first five are listed below—but may also contain extras such as ginger or coriander. It should be very fragrant, with star anise dominating.

1 teaspoon Szechuan peppercorns, black seeds discarded

1 whole star anise

¾ teaspoon fennel seeds

½ teaspoon whole cloves (about 10)

2 pieces cinnamon stick or cassia bark, about 2 inches long

¼ teaspoon ground ginger

Put the Szechuan peppercorns into a dry skillet and toast briefly. Using a spice grinder or mortar and pestle, grind the peppercorns, star anise, fennel seeds, cloves, and cinnamon, then stir in the ground ginger. Store in an airtight container.

Chinese Master Sauce Spices

Master sauce is a dark, spiced soy-based Chinese sauce used for cooking chicken, duck, pork, and even fish. It is used several times, becoming more mature and desirable with each use (see Red-Cooked Chicken, page 110.) The spices can vary a little, but the mix must include star anise, cinnamon sticks, and cloves. Other ingredients can include licorice root, orange or tangerine zest, fennel seeds, ginger, and Szechuan peppercorns, depending on the dish.

Chinese Red Chile Oil

Though chiles are not as prevalent in East Asia as in other parts of the continent, this is one of the most popular Chinese condiments. The longer the red pepper flakes are left in the oil, the hotter it will be.

1 cup peanut oil

1 tablespoon hot red pepper flakes

Heat the oil in a saucepan, stir in the pepper flakes, and let cool completely. Pour into a clean bottle, seal, and use. Regional variations can be made by adding ½ small onion, chopped, or 2 tablespoons Asian dried shrimp.

Japanese Pickled Ginger

A favorite Japanese accompaniment for sushi and sashimi, this is becoming widely available in larger supermarkets and Asian food stores. It is easy to make, and the result is a real palate cleanser.

4 inches fresh ginger, peeled and very thinly sliced with a mandoline, grater, or sharp cleaver

a pinch of sea salt

6 tablespoons Japanese rice vinegar

1 tablespoon sugar

sterilized preserving jar with seal or glass bottle with tight-fitting lid

Put the ginger into a small bowl, sprinkle with salt, and toss well. Put the vinegar, sugar, and water into a bowl and mix well, then pour it over the ginger slices and mix again. Transfer to the sterilized jar, making sure the ginger is covered with the liquid. Seal tightly and store in the refrigerator for at least 3 days, or up to 1 week.

Japanese Wasabi Paste

Wasabi paste is available in tubes. It is often a bright lime green color, but the color changes after opening, so don't keep opened tubes longer than a few days. Aficionados prefer to make their own paste from wasabi powder, and the finest quality is very pale indeed.

1 tablespoon wasabi powder

Put the powder into a small tea bowl or eggcup, add a dash of water, and stir with a chopstick. Serve with sushi, sashimi, and other Japanese dishes. To eat, the paste is often stirred into a small dipping bowl of shoyu (Japanese soy sauce).

Japanese Shichimi Togarashi

A ubiquitous Japanese spice mix, widely available in supermarkets. This blend of seven spices includes the unusual flavors of sansho, yuzo (dried citrus peel), and nori (dried seaweed). Sprinkle over soups such as miso (page 107). Sometimes other seeds such as hemp or rape are used, as well as shisho, a herb with a serrated leaf.

½ teaspoon white or black poppy seeds

½ teaspoon black sesame seeds

1 teaspoon white sesame seeds

1 teaspoon chili powder

1½–2 teaspoons ground sansho

1½ teaspoons dried yuzo flakes

few pieces of nori or mixed dried sea vegetables such as dulse and sea lettuce, crushed

Put all the ingredients into an airtight container, stir well, then store in a cool, dark place.

southeast asia

How can one easily categorize the cuisine of a region as ethnically diverse as Southeast Asia? For 2000 years or more, it has been a melting pot of peoples, religions, and spices, and from early times was the very source and hub of much of the spice trade for the rest of the world.

In almost every corner of the region, cooks have a predilection for spice pastes or, more appropriately, spice, herb, and fish pastes, as they incorporate all of these and a wide array of other ingredients. People make use of many indigenous spices but, above all, one that isn't native at all, the chile, brought by the Portuguese all the way from the New World—the long way round.

As in other parts of Asia, the combination of spices varies from region to region, and from household to household. Pastes can be full of bright herby fragrance, such as those of Thailand, Laos, Cambodia, and Vietnam, or heavier, like those of Burma, Malaysia, or Indonesia, perhaps betraying an ancient Indian influence.

Turmeric, cumin, coriander, and peppercorns sit alongside a panoply of lesser-known root spices and herbs. Rhizomes such as galangal and zedoary contribute their individual fragrance, while torch ginger—a beautiful wild ginger bud—and the long rhizome Chinese keys (lesser galangal, kencur, or krachai) are used in salads or eaten raw with dips. But, above all, there are chiles, chiles, and more chiles.

the spice islands of nutmeg and cloves

Cockatoos, lorikeets, and nutmeg pigeons abound on a mini-archipelago so otherworldly that those who once sought its riches scarcely believed this magical place existed. Collectively known as the Moluccas (today Maluku), this group of Indonesian islands is the original home of cloves, nutmeg, and mace, the holy trinity of spices. To the swashbuckling adventurers, profiteers, and colonizers from three continents who eventually found these fabled Spice Islands, they proved to be as extraordinary as they had imagined.

The heady fragrance of nutmeg and mace hovers over the Banda Islands in the south, while a few hundred miles north lie the two most important clove islands, Ternate and Tidore. Just as vital was an area further west, the port of Malacca (now Melaka), built in 1402 on the Malay Peninsula. Its position on the Straits of Malacca, a speedy route between the Indian Ocean and South China Sea, guaranteed its hold over Asian and eventually European trade to and from the Spice Islands.

There was a spice trade from earliest times—with other islands, the Malay Peninsula, Arabia, Persia, India, and China from at least 300 BC and perhaps earlier.

The trade wasn't all one way. Pepper from India's Malabar Coast was naturalized in Sumatra and Java from this time, becoming another vital export. Rulers in Java and Sumatra held control of the straits, and in the seventh century, the glorious Buddhist Sriwijaya kingdom arose. Sumatran merchants regularly set sail for China, one of the kingdom's most important trading contacts. Meanwhile, in the Moluccas, Ternate and Tidore grew into wealthy sultanates after the arrival of Islam, wielding great power over lesser clove islands.

The nobility and various merchant communities capitalized on this prosperity, developing a rich and varied exchange of goods such as silk, birds of paradise plumage, porcelain, cotton, bronze, jewels, and spices. When the port of Malacca was first built—by the exiled Sumatran Hindu Prince Parameshwara—traders from many lands settled in this golden city, which became a thriving emporium of spices from East and West.

This was an amazing time for all of Asia. China too looked outward for a short time, as Zheng He (page 101) undertook the first of several expeditions. He took his massive trading junks and support boats to Sumatra, Java, Siam, and, especially, Malacca. With the junks came lavish gifts and the founding of strong trading links with China. As a result, Malacca saw an influx of Chinese settlers who left their culinary legacy, especially in Singapore's Nonya cooking.

Witnessing this prosperity, Europe came up with the axiom "Whoever is Lord of Malacca has his hands on the throat of Venice …," and thus began the European bid for the port and dominance over the Spice Islands. By this time, Malacca was an Islamic kingdom, but fell in 1511 to Portugal, raising the ire of its arch-rival Spain. The Portuguese sent fleets to the Banda, then captured and eventually built a fort on the clove island of Ternate, while its rival Tidore was briefly in the hands of Spain. Ancient feuds between the two islands did much to dislodge both European powers— although Portugal lasted longest, around 65 years. A brief period of respite came under Ternate's Sultan Baab who had ousted the Portuguese in 1575. Sadly, it was a short-lived victory; the European arrival had changed the face of the Moluccas forever.

Britain entered the East Indies late in the game, but established its first

colony in the world in 1603 on the tiny but important nutmeg island of Run, which became a point of bitter dispute between the English and the far more ambitious Dutch.

By 1595, the Dutch had entered the fray, and neither the Indonesians nor the other colonial nations could have foreseen their endurance. Formed in 1602, their Vereenigde Oost-Indische Compagnie (VOC) quickly established plantations on a few closely guarded islands, callously ridding the others of their valuable crops, to emerge as the most powerful contender in the Spice Island game. With absolute efficiency and fearsome tactics, by the second half of the century, VOC had become the richest company in the world.

Despite the devastation of the Moluccas after the European conquest, there are some stories that stand out for their humanity and affection. The tales of Magellan's comrade Francisco Serrão and Sir Francis Drake's visits to the islands remain ever endearing. Serrão led the mission from Malacca to the Moluccas, where his ship ran aground on Ternate. Surprised to receive a warm and regal reception, he fell absolutely head over heels in love with the island. He was held captive by

the splendor and sophistication of the court, the tropical air and the handsome, friendly people. Despite incurring the wrath of his countrymen for not sailing back to Malacca and for cavorting with Muslim subjects, Serrão found every excuse to stay as valued ambassador to the Sultan and he eventually married a royal Moluccan princess. His letters to his great friend Magellan reflected his total submission to this volcanic home of cloves, as he urged Magellan to "join him in paradise." This correspondence spurred on the great navigator, although both adventurers were killed before they could retire together on fragrant Ternate.

Sir Francis Drake, the naval hero of Elizabethan England, enjoyed a brief sojourn that made history. His arrival in the Spice Islands in 1579 met with an equally joyous welcome by that same Sultan Baab of Ternate. Both Drake on his ship and the Sultan with his floating entourage pleased each other with deferential gestures and all-round goodwill. The Sultan did so with eastern etiquette and royal style, while Drake responded with cannon fire and pomp-filled trumpet music. The king so enjoyed the display that he asked that his boat be attached to the stern as Drake's ship floated around with music

spilling out across the water. The simple visit ended as peacefully as it had begun, with Drake buying all the spices he wanted and returning to England a hero, while the Sultan went back to his happy isle. Not all was ill will in those battle-filled days.

Portuguese romantics and English gentlemen aside, it was not until the late 18th century that the Dutch saw the decline of their mighty company. A daring Frenchman smuggled the spices out to the Indian Ocean islands, and the clove, nutmeg, and mace monopoly was broken forever. No longer would such spices depend upon the ambitions of one country, but on the markets of the world.

Above, from left: The beautiful Hindu island of Bali is a tiny remnant of the great Hindu kingdoms which once ruled in Indonesia, controlling the Straits of Malacca and the spice trade • Nuóc cham is the ubiquitous spicy Vietnamese dipping sauce (page 127) found on every home and restaurant table. Chiles, though not native to the area, have taken over from ginger and pepper as the favorite hot spice • In Indonesia, spicy sambals are served with almost every meal. Somewhere between a relish and a salad, they add flavor and fire to other dishes.

vegetarian cashew salad
with tamarind dressing

8 leaves of Napa cabbage

1 large carrot

1 cucumber, about 8 inches long, halved, seeded, cut into 2-inch sections, then finely sliced lengthwise

6 scallions, sliced diagonally

8 slices dried mango, chopped

1/2 cup cashews, toasted in a dry skillet, then coarsely crushed

Tamarind dressing*

2 oz. lump tamarind (an apricot-size piece), or about 2 teaspoons tamarind concentrate, to taste

1/2 teaspoon Szechuan peppercorns, lightly toasted in a dry skillet, then coarsely crushed

2 teaspoons toasted sesame oil

1 garlic clove, finely chopped

1/2 teaspoon brown or palm sugar, to taste

about 2 tablespoons chopped Thai basil, Vietnamese mint, or cilantro

sea salt

Serves 4

*You can substitute the similar but thicker Vietnamese Tamarind Dip (page 137) for this dressing.

A simple vegetarian salad with fragrant Southeast Asian flavors—Vietnamese and Thai—but with a hint of Chinese also. It is versatile too, because other ingredients can be added according to the season or the tastes of your guests. Sour tamarind and Szechuan pepper form an unusual partnership in the dressing—a combination of sour and hot. Tamarind is available in lump form, or as a ready-to-use concentrate. Although the latter is very handy, making your own from the lump of seeds and fibers is easy and the freshness is hard to beat.

To make the tamarind water for the dressing, put the tamarind into a small glass bowl. Add 1 cup warm water and let soak for 15 minutes. Then squeeze the tamarind through your fingers in the water and continue until all of it has been squeezed into a pulp. Press through a strainer.

Put 1/3 cup of the strained tamarind water, the Szechuan pepper, sesame oil, garlic, sugar, and chopped herbs into a screw-top bottle and shake well. Set aside. (Any remaining tamarind water can be boiled in a pan, let cool, then refrigerated for later use.)

Stack the Napa cabbage leaves on top of each other and slice them finely. Grate the carrot into long sticks using the large blade of a box grater, or slice finely into long strips. Divide the shredded leaves between 4 plates, add a layer of grated carrot, then the cucumber strips. Top with the scallions and dried mango. Sprinkle the dressing over the salad, top with the cashews, then serve.

Variations

• Instead of Napa cabbage leaves, use other crisp leaves such as romaine.

• Omit the leaves and make a simple carrot and scallion salad.

• For a non-vegetarian version, add 2 poached boneless skinless chicken breasts, cooled and pulled into shreds, or 2 duck breasts, cooked in a stove-top grill pan, then sliced.

stir-fried peanut shrimp
with cilantro noodles

6 oz. rice stick noodles

5 tablespoons peanut oil

a pinch of ground coriander

2 kaffir lime leaves, 1 finely sliced or crushed and 1 left whole

1 stalk of lemongrass, outer leaves discarded, the remainder very finely chopped

3–4 red bird's eye chiles, seeded and finely sliced

3 scallions, chopped

1 large garlic clove, crushed

2 cups prepared stir-fry vegetables, such as broccoli and cauliflower florets, red bell pepper strips, asparagus tips, sliced onion, sugar snap peas, string beans, all cut into bite-size pieces

a pinch of sugar

3 tablespoons Thai fish sauce (nam pla)

8 oz. uncooked, shelled jumbo shrimp, deveined (about 14 oz., with the shell on)

freshly squeezed juice of 1 lemon

1 cup dry-roasted peanuts, coarsely ground

about 2 tablespoons peanut oil

¾ cup finely chopped fresh cilantro

To serve

a handful of cilantro leaves, chopped

a few green bird's eye chiles, seeded and finely sliced

2 scallions, green part only, finely sliced

a handful of bean sprouts

Serves 4

Similar to the popular dish Pad Thai, this recipe is dryer, less sweet, and omits certain key ingredients such as eggs, substituting stir-fry vegetables instead. Tiny, blindingly hot bird's eye chiles are an essential spice in Southeast Asian cuisine: if you would prefer this dish less hot, use another kind of chile or reduce the number.

Put the noodles into a bowl and cover with boiling water. Let soak for 4 minutes or according to the instructions on the package. Drain, return to the bowl, and cover with cold water until ready to serve. Have a kettle of boiling water ready to reheat.

Put 3 tablespoons of the oil into a nonstick wok, heat well and swirl to coat. Add the ground coriander, kaffir lime leaves, lemongrass, red chiles, and chopped scallions and stir-fry briefly. Add the garlic and stir-fry again for 20 seconds. Add the prepared vegetables, sugar, and 2 tablespoons of the fish sauce and stir-fry over medium-high heat for 1 minute.

Add the shrimp and lemon juice and stir-fry for 1 minute, then add half the ground peanuts. Mix well, add the remaining tablespoon of fish sauce, and cook for 2 more minutes or until the shrimp turn pink.

Meanwhile, drain the noodles again and return them to the bowl. Cover with boiling water, drain, and return to the bowl. Add 2 tablespoons peanut oil, toss to coat, add the cilantro, and toss again. Add the noodles to the wok, toss to coat, then serve immediately topped with cilantro, green chiles, scallions, bean sprouts, and the remaining peanuts.

2 tablespoons peanut oil

1 recipe Laksa Spice Paste (Southeast Asian Spice Mixes, page 136)

1½ quarts chicken stock

1 stalk of lemongrass, halved lengthwise

2 kaffir lime leaves (optional)

2 long sprigs of lemon balm (optional)

4 thin slices of fresh ginger or galangal

1 teaspoon light soy sauce

1¾ cups canned coconut milk

1 lb. uncooked shrimp, shelled and deveined

4 oz. (about 1 cup) bean sprouts, rinsed and trimmed

brown sugar or palm sugar, to taste

sea salt

a bunch of cilantro, chopped

To serve

8 oz. thick Chinese egg noodles, freshly cooked and drained

4 inches cucumber, seeded and sliced into matchstick strips

a few lemon balm leaves, finely sliced (optional)

a handful of shredded Napa cabbage

Serves 4–6

Laksa, the spicy shrimp and noodle soup from Malaysia and Singapore, has become fashionable all over the world. This one is a speciality of the Nonya or Straits-Chinese community. Its bright yellow color comes from turmeric and, on its home ground, fresh turmeric is often used rather than the ground turmeric found in the West. The fresh version is often sold in Southeast Asian and Indian markets: it looks like orange ginger (page 75) and is prepared in the same way— peeled and grated. Use about 1 inch to equal 1 teaspoon dried ground turmeric.

The ingredients vary according to region and what's available in the market— in Malaysia, local ingredients like the fragrant laksa leaf and wild ginger bud may also be added. A little creative license is called for, so try my suggestions or think of your own, within reason!

laksa lemak
singapore turmeric noodle soup

Heat the oil in a large saucepan and add the laksa paste. Sauté for about 8 minutes. Add the chicken stock, lemongrass, lime leaves, lemon balm, if using, ginger or galangal, and soy sauce. Bring to a boil and add the coconut milk, stirring to keep it from separating. Reduce the heat and simmer gently for 15 minutes.

Add the shrimp, bean sprouts, sugar, and salt. Simmer for 2–3 minutes, until the shrimp are just cooked. Discard the lemon balm and lemongrass and add the chopped cilantro.

To serve, put the noodles, cucumber, lemon balm, if using, and Napa cabbage into 4 large or 6 smaller bowls, then ladle in the soup.

Note Turmeric, being a strong spice, is usually used sparingly as a natural coloring. However, in laksa it plays a starring role. Malays sometimes add up to 2 teaspoons, but I have reduced the quantity in the paste so that turmeric does not overpower the soup. I like this soup best when the broth, minus the shrimp, is left for an hour or more, for the flavors to mingle and mellow—delicious. Add the shrimp just before you are ready to serve. Do not use ready-cooked shrimp: their tough texture will spoil the laksa.

vietnamese spiced squid

Vietnam is known for its delicate cuisine combined with some of the more assertive flavors associated with Southeast Asia. It is notable for its great use of herbs, while spices, when used, are balanced and often gentle. However in southern cooking, typical spices such as star anise, tamarind, chiles, galangal, ginger, and occasionally turmeric, five-spice powder, and curry powder appear in various dishes. This delicious appetizer of stuffed baby squid, spiced with a little star anise, ginger, and pepper, is a fine example of Vietnamese cuisine. Nuóc cham is the traditional spicy Vietnamese dipping sauce, but you could use soy sauce or chile sauce.

1 oz. cellophane rice noodles (rice vermicelli), about 1 small bundle

1/2 cup peanut oil

3 scallions, chopped

1 inch fresh ginger, peeled and grated

2 garlic cloves, chopped

16 prepared, cleaned baby squid with tentacles reserved*

12 oz. ground pork

2–3 "petals" of 1 star anise, finely crushed (about 1/4 teaspoon ground)

1/4 teaspoon cracked black pepper

1 tablespoon Thai or Vietnamese fish sauce

a pinch of sugar

a pinch of sea salt

a handful of mixed Asian herbs, to serve

Nuóc cham dipping sauce

1 garlic clove, crushed

1 red bird's eye chile, finely sliced

2 tablespoons sugar

freshly squeezed juice of 1/2 lime

1/4 cup fish sauce

Makes 16

To make the dipping sauce, use a mortar and pestle to grind the garlic, chile, and sugar to form a paste. Stir in the lime juice, fish sauce, and about 3 tablespoons water. Transfer to a dipping bowl.

To prepare the stuffing, pour boiling water over the noodles and let soak for 4 minutes or according to the instructions on the package. Drain well, coarsely chop the noodles, and transfer to a large bowl.

Put 1 tablespoon of the peanut oil into a wok, heat well, swirl to coat, then add the scallions, ginger, and garlic. Stir-fry for a few minutes until softened, then add to the bowl. Chop the squid tentacles and add to the ingredients in the bowl. Add the pork, star anise, pepper, fish sauce, sugar, and salt and mix well.

Stuff the squid bodies, leaving a little space at the top. Secure closed with toothpicks.

Heat the remaining oil in a skillet and add the squid. Cook gently for 10–12 minutes, until lightly browned in places and cooked through.

Slice the squid or leave them whole, then serve with the fresh herbs and nuóc cham or other Southeast Asian dipping sauce.

*Note To prepare the squid, cut off the tentacles and chop them coarsely. Cut off and discard the eye sections. Rinse out the bodies, discarding the tiny transparent quill. If you can't find squid with tentacles, buy an extra body, chop it coarsely, then add to the stuffing mixture.

thai green chicken curry

2 cans coconut milk, 14 oz. each

1 recipe Thai Green Curry Paste
(Southeast Asian Spice Mixes, page 136)
or 7 tablespoons store-bought paste

4 boneless skinless chicken breasts,
thickly sliced

2 tablespoons Thai fish sauce

¼ teaspoon brown sugar or palm sugar

To serve

Thai basil leaves or chopped cilantro

1 lime, cut into 4 wedges

3 bird's eye chiles, halved lengthwise
(optional)

Serves 4

This famous Thai curry is full of the fragrance of fresh spices and herbs for which Thai cuisine is known. Coconut milk tempers the heat of the tiny bird's eye chiles in the green curry paste (although this is a mild version) and adds the essential creaminess.

Throughout Southeast Asia, although dried spices are certainly used, the fresh versions are more typical. The spice trade grew out of the desire, especially in Europe, for the flavors of Asian spices. These were mostly used fresh in their own countries, but they could only be exported in their dry form. Modern modes of transport and polytunnel agriculture mean that fresh chiles, ginger, and similar spices are available in almost every supermarket.

Put a ladle of the the coconut milk into a wok or deep skillet, add the curry paste, and stir-fry to release the aromas. Add the chicken and stir-fry to coat with the spices. Add the remaining coconut milk, bring to a boil, reduce the heat, and simmer gently for about 8 minutes, or until the chicken is cooked through and still tender.

Add the fish sauce and sugar and cook for a further 1 minute. Transfer to a serving bowl, sprinkle with the herbs, add the lime wedges, then serve with other Thai dishes and fragrant Thai rice.

Note Thais usually serve all dishes at once. Steamed rice is the basis of the meal, and diners take a share of each dish to eat with rice. One dish is eaten at a time—never several at once. A fork and spoon is used, with the fork being used to push the food onto the spoon.

thai mussaman beef curry

¾ cup raw peanuts

1¾ lb. cubed steak

1¼ teaspoons tamarind concentrate or a few tablespoons tamarind water (page 121)

2 cans coconut milk, 14 oz. each

1 large potato, chopped into large chunks

sea salt or fish sauce

Mussaman spice paste

2 cardamom pods

½ cinnamon stick

1 teaspoon cumin seeds

1½ tablespoons coriander seeds

½ teaspoon freshly grated nutmeg

5 red bird's eye chiles, seeded and chopped

1 stalk of lemongrass, outer leaves discarded, the remainder very finely chopped

4 garlic cloves, chopped

4 small Thai shallots, coarsely chopped

3 tablespoons chopped cilantro stems or roots

1 tiny piece of shrimp paste, toasted, (see note page 134), or 1 teaspoon anchovy paste

Serves 6

This unusual Thai curry is characterized by its thick, peanut sauce and the kind of spicing more commonly identified with Malay or Indonesian cooking. Yet it is a firm favorite, inside and outside Thailand. I've eaten this dish from Seattle to Boston and from Dhahran to Cardiff! As it is exceedingly rich, serve in smaller portions than you would your average curry. Serve with rice, a fresh Thai salad, or any light Southeast Asian side dishes (see note page 128).

Put the peanuts into a dry skillet and toast until aromatic. Transfer to a clean dish towel and rub together. Their skins should slip off easily. Using a mortar and pestle or food processor, grind the peanuts coarsely and set aside.

Put the beef into a large, heavy saucepan, add 2 cups water and bring to a boil. Reduce the heat and simmer for about 1½ hours. Add sea salt or fish sauce, to taste.

To make the spice paste, put the cardamom, cinnamon, cumin, and coriander seeds into a dry skillet and toast until aromatic. Using a blender or mortar and pestle, grind to a fine powder. Add the nutmeg, chiles, lemongrass, garlic, shallots, cilantro stems or roots, and shrimp paste and grind to a thick paste, adding a little water if necessary.

Remove the beef from the saucepan and set aside. The liquid will be substantially reduced, so take care not to let the dish burn at this last stage. You should stir frequently and keep the heat low.

Add the tamarind and half the spice paste and stir. (Freeze the remaining paste for future use.) Stir the coconut milk into the sauce. Return the beef to the saucepan, then add the potatoes—if the mixture is looking too dry, add a little extra water. Simmer gently for 20 minutes, stirring frequently. Stir in the peanuts and cook for another 1–2 minutes.

burmese pork hinleh

3 tablespoons peanut or safflower oil

1½ lb. well trimmed boneless sparerib, sliced into chunks*

2 cups beef stock

Hinleh (curry) paste

4–6 red bird's eye chiles, seeded and chopped

5 garlic cloves, quartered

½ onion, coarsely chopped

2 inches fresh ginger, peeled and grated

¼ teaspoon ground turmeric

2 inches fresh galangal, peeled and grated (see recipe introduction)

1 stalk of lemongrass, outer leaves discarded, the remainder very finely chopped

3 anchovies in oil, drained and finely chopped plus a dash of fish sauce, or ½ teaspoon dried shrimp paste, toasted (see note, page 134)

To serve

a handful of Thai basil or cilantro

2 red bird's eye chiles, finely sliced lengthwise

boiled rice

Serves 4

This curry is a Burmese specialty and doesn't include the coconut milk so typical of Southeast Asian cooking. It does use three root spices from the same family—turmeric, ginger, and galangal. In Burma and throughout Asia, all three are used fresh, but in the West, turmeric is rarely available fresh, so the ground form must be used instead. If you can't get fresh galangal, use extra fresh ginger instead (a pity, because galangal's bright flavor is delicious).

To make the hinleh paste, put all the ingredients into a blender and grind to a paste, adding a dash of water to let the blades run. Alternatively, use a mortar and pestle.

Heat the oil in a large saucepan and add the paste. Stir-fry for several minutes. Add the pork and stir-fry to seal. Add the stock, bring to a boil, reduce the heat, and simmer gently, stirring occasionally, for 40–45 minutes until cooked through but very tender. Sprinkle with the herbs and chile and serve with rice.

*Note I prefer boneless sparerib meat, which takes longer to cook, but doesn't dry out as easily as leg meat. It gives best results at a lower temperature. Otherwise, you can also use the best cut—filet or tenderloin—for tender, fast cooking meat.

indonesian beef and coconut soup

1½ lb. trimmed stewing beef, cut into small chunks

7 white peppercorns

1 inch fresh galangal, peeled and sliced, or fresh ginger

1 teaspoon freshly grated nutmeg

¼ teaspoon ground turmeric

1 can coconut milk, 14 oz.

sea salt

Spice paste

2–3 tablespoons peanut oil

1 teaspoon ground coriander

7 white peppercorns

4 red bird's eye chiles

2 teaspoons brown or palm sugar

1 garlic clove, chopped

5 fresh Thai basil (or sweet basil) leaves

a large handful of fresh cilantro, about 1 oz., coarsely chopped

8 pink Thai shallots or 1 regular shallot

a few cardamom seeds (not pods)

1 inch fresh ginger, peeled and chopped

a small piece of shrimp paste*, toasted in a dry skillet or a hot oven, or 1 teaspoon anchovy paste mixed with 1 tablespoon fish sauce

Serves 4–6

This strongly spiced and flavored soup has slices of meat swimming in plenty of creamy broth. It is quintessentially Indonesian in its spicing, influenced by the nation's diverse population and topography. Wave after wave of settlers entered Indonesia long ago, from Malays, Indians, and Chinese to Arab traders. Living on the world's largest archipelago and comprising around 350 ethnic groups, Indonesians are a varied people and so is their cuisine. What comes across in dishes like this soup is a fascinating mixture of spices and flavors.

Put all the spice paste ingredients into a blender or a food processor and grind to a thick paste, adding a dash of water to let the blades run. Set aside.

Put the beef, peppercorns, galangal, nutmeg, turmeric, and salt into a saucepan, add 1½ quarts water and bring to a boil, skimming off the foam as it rises to the surface. Stir, reduce the heat, and simmer uncovered for about 1½ hours, until the meat is mostly tender and the stock is well reduced.

Strain the beef, discarding the galangal slices and peppercorns, but reserving the beef and stock. Return the stock to the pan, then stir in the spice paste. Bring to a boil, reduce the heat, add the beef, and simmer for 5 minutes, stirring regularly.

Finally, add the coconut milk and simmer gently for a few minutes. Serve the soup on its own or with a small mound of plain rice. You could also serve it with an Indonesian spiced rice like nasi goreng, but the soup should then be eaten separately.

*Note Dried shrimp paste is also known as trassi, beluchan, or blachan. Extremely pungent, it gives a distinctive taste to South-east Asian food and is worth hunting down in a Thai/Malay/Indonesian food store. Use a very small piece (about ½ teaspoon) and always toast it before using. Wrap it in a small piece of foil and cook in a hot oven until it darkens—a few minutes per side. I recommend opening your windows when using shrimp paste—it leaves a pervasive scent in your kitchen!

southeast asian spice mixes

Southeast Asian spice mixes and pastes are a subtle blend of salt and sweet, sour and spicy. Especially spicy. The Asian penchant for fire began with ginger, galangal, and pepper, but when the chile arrived, everything changed. Now the variety and sheer heat of Asian chiles is staggering. Because spices in this region are usually fresh, the mixtures are often in paste or liquid form.

Thai Green Curry Paste

This mild green curry paste is made from spices and herbs; if you wish to be true to its roots, feel free to use many more chiles.

1 tablespoon grated kaffir lime zest or regular lime zest

4–5 green bird's eye chiles, seeded and chopped

several lemon balm leaves (optional), chopped

1 stalk of lemongrass, outer leaves discarded, the remainder very finely chopped

¾ teaspoon coriander seeds, toasted in a dry skillet

a handful of cilantro leaves, chopped

a handful of cilantro stems and roots, chopped

2–3 garlic cloves, chopped

2 scallions, chopped

1 inch fresh galangal or ginger, peeled and chopped

3 tablespoons Thai fish sauce

Using a blender or mortar and pestle, grind all the ingredients to a thick, chunky paste. If using a blender, add a little water to let the blades run.

Thai Red Curry Paste

This paste is fierce in color and heat (decrease or increase the chiles according to taste).

8–10 red bird's eye chiles, seeded and chopped

a small piece of dried shrimp paste, toasted in a dry skillet or hot oven, or 1 teaspoon anchovy paste plus a dash of Thai fish sauce (page 134)

1 tablespoon grated kaffir lime or regular lime zest

1 stalk of lemongrass, outer leaves discarded, the remainder very finely chopped

1 teaspoon cumin seeds, toasted in a dry skillet

1 teaspoon white or black peppercorns

1 tablespoon coriander seeds, toasted in a dry skillet

2–3 garlic cloves, chopped

1 inch fresh galangal or ginger, peeled and chopped

3 tablespoons chopped shallots or onions

1–2 tablespoons finely chopped cilantro root

Follow the method for Thai Green Curry Paste, above.

Laksa Paste

The essential spice paste for Laksa Lemak, one of the great soups of Southeast Asia—a speciality of the Chinese-Malay Nonya community of Singapore.

6 shallots, coarsely chopped

4 red chiles, seeded and chopped

1 stalk of lemongrass, outer leaves discarded, the remainder very finely chopped

1 teaspoon ground turmeric

1 garlic clove, chopped

½ teaspoon ground ginger or galangal

a tiny piece of shrimp paste, toasted,
or ½ teaspoon anchovy paste

6 macadamia nuts or 12 almonds

1 kaffir lime leaf (optional)

2 tablespoons Thai fish sauce

Follow the method for Thai Green Curry
Paste, above.

Indonesian Sambal

This is just one example of the huge
family of fiery Indonesian condiments.
The number of chiles may sound
daunting, but seeding reduces their
heat. I've also substituted common red
chiles for the traditional small, fearsome
bird's eye variety. Use fewer chiles if
you prefer or, if you like fiery foods, use
bird's eyes instead.

15 red chiles, seeded and chopped

2 tomatoes, halved

10 small shallots, preferably pink Thai

8 cashews

2 garlic cloves, chopped

1 inch fresh galangal or ginger, peeled and
chopped

a small piece of dried shrimp paste, toasted
in a dry skillet or hot oven

1 tablespoon brown or palm sugar

3 tablespoons peanut oil

2 tablespoons freshly squeezed lemon juice

sea salt, to taste

Using a blender or mortar and pestle,
grind all the ingredients to a paste.
Serve as a condiment.

Vietnamese Tamarind Dip

This Southeast Asian dip has a
wonderful sour flavor that can only

come from tamarind. You could also
use this as a dressing—try it instead of
the thinner dressing on page 121.

3 oz. lump tamarind (the size of 3 apricots)
or 1 teaspoon tamarind concentrate

2 teaspoons peanut oil

1–2 teaspoons Vietnamese/Thai fish sauce

1 large garlic clove, crushed

1 teaspoon brown or palm sugar

a dash of fresh lime juice (optional)

To prepare the lump tamarind, put it
into a small bowl. Add ¾ cup hot water
and let soak for 15 minutes. Squeeze
the tamarind through your fingers in the
water and continue until all of it has
been squeezed into a pulp. Press
through a strainer.

Put 3 tablespoons of the prepared
tamarind, or the 1 teaspoon
concentrate into a small bowl, beat in
the peanut oil and fish sauce, add the
garlic and sugar, and stir until
dissolved. Add a dash of lime juice if
using, then serve.

(Boil any remaining prepared tamarind,
let cool and refrigerate for later use.)

spice tips

Buying Spices If possible, buy whole spices and grind them yourself. They last much longer and you will know they're fresh. However, most of us buy some ground spices for ease. I buy spice in "ethnic" stores because they're less expensive, and if you use spices regularly, such stores supply them in larger quantities than supermarkets. Even some commercially blended spices can be of good quality in the former—especially handy for blends that include arcane spices. For the most part, however, it is always best to grind your own blends. If spices are sold loose, as in some specialty shops, take advantage, as you can smell and judge whether they are fresh or old.

Storing Spices Store spices in airtight jars— glass bottles are perfect. Ground spices stored thus will last a few months; to keep them longer, refrigerate or freeze. Some spices, like fresh ginger or galangal won't keep for very long, so slice, seal, and freeze. To use, pour a little boiling water over a slice and leave for a few minutes. Lump tamarind keeps for a long time, while tamarind concentrate will have an expiration date on the bottle.

Grinding Spices I use a coffee grinder, blender, or food processor. The nut mill attachment on a blender is also good. For pastes, the grinding stones of the East are perfect (page 74), as is a mortar and pestle.

Bruising and Toasting Spices Some whole spices are bruised before use, to release aroma and flavor. Toasting spices is essential for many recipes and brings out the best flavor. Toast spices for just 1–2 minutes over low heat as they burn easily. You will smell their scent when they're ready. Sometimes, especially in South Asia, a drop of oil is heated in the pan before toasting. Before grinding, let the spices cool and dry.

Cooking with Spices and Spice Pastes Spices are used in many ways. Whole spices may be added directly to stocks and soups or they may be "tempered" in hot oil first. Ground spice mixtures can be added directly to a dish at different times; prior to cooking as in a marinade, or a few minutes before a dish is served. Spice pastes range from simple to complex and are usually stir-fried in hot oil before other ingredients are added. Cook over low heat so they do not burn—often, a drop of water is added to stop them sticking. For best results, follow these general rules as well as individual recipe methods.

spice directory

Allspice (*Pimenta dioica*)
Native to the Caribbean and Central America. Its name reflects its fruity, peppery mixture of clove, nutmeg, and cinnamon flavors; also known as Jamaica pepper. Allspice is a brown-red berry used in pickles, marinades, soups, and stews. Ground, it is used to season meats and is a component of European mixed spice. For cakes, cookies, and desserts.

Anise/Aniseed (*Pimpinella anisum*) and Fennel (*Foeniculum vulgare*)
Native to the Mediterranean region. Botanically related, both have small, pale gray-green, ridged seeds with licorice flavor; anise is sweeter than fennel. Since anise has such a distinctive flavor, a number of other spices are described as having an "anise" note. In Europe they flavor pastis, ouzo, and other anise-based drinks. Aniseed is used in baked goods and confectionery, while fennel is particularly good with fish and pork.

Caraway (*Carum carvi*)
Native to Asia and northern and central Europe. Caraway is often confused with cumin but has a stronger anise note, especially when cooked. In Europe the small, thin brown seeds are used to flavor pickles, sauerkraut, cabbage dishes, bread, and cheese; great with sour cream. Also popular in Turkey, and used in harissa in Tunisia.

Cardamom (*Elettaria cardamomum*)
Native to southern India and Sri Lanka. A "luxury" spice with a unique, exotic scent. Pale green oval pods (white cardamoms are bleached green ones) with tiny black seeds; brown cardamom is a different species (see page 140). Whole pods may be used, bruised to release the scent, or just the seeds—whole or ground to a powder. (Whole pods are also crushed to a powder, but that of the seeds alone is "sweeter"). Used extensively in South Asia in both sweet and savory dishes, alone or in spice mixtures; also popular in the Middle East, where it is used as coffee flavoring, and in Finnish baking.

Cassia (*Cinnamomum cassia*)
Native to China. The Latin name reflects its similarity to true cinnamon, although cassia is not as delicate or sweetly scented. Often sold as broken pieces of bark, or ground to a powder. Widely used in China, Southeast Asia, and the United States.

Chile, Paprika (*Capsicum annuum, C. chinense, C. frutescens*)
Native to Central and South America and the Caribbean; most of the world's chile cultivars descend from the above species. Pods vary in color, shape, and size: red, orange, green; long and thin or bonnet-shaped; 1–8 inches; strength ranges from mild to fierce. Seeds can be removed to reduce ferocity. Dried chiles may be sold whole, crushed, or ground to a powder; cayenne pepper is a fiery variety, paprika is milder. Hungarian paprika and the smoked Spanish version (pimentón) are superior to most commercial paprika. There are two kinds of pimentón; hot and sweet. They are both oak-smoked, the best supposedly being produced in Extremadura. Sold in small square cans with resealable lids to seal in flavor and scent.

Cinnamon (*Cinnamomum verum* or *C. zeylanicum*)
Native to Sri Lanka (formerly Ceylon). The brown "quills" are the rolled-up inner bark of an evergreen tree, used whole or ground. Prized around the world for its sweet woody fragrance and taste. Cinnamon graces sweet foods in the West; elsewhere it enriches savory foods, from tagines to biryanis.

Cloves (*Eugenia caryophyllus, Syzygium aromaticum*)
Native to the Maluku Islands (formerly Moluccas), Indonesia. Cloves are the unopened flower buds of an evergreen tree, dried and used whole or ground, as well as in spice mixtures. Dark reddish-brown with a sultry scent and slightly bitter flavor—numbing when tasted alone. Used in baking and in savory foods: in pulows, pressed into onions to flavor stocks or stews, or into hams before they are baked.

Coriander (*Coriandrum sativum*)
Native to the Mediterranean and West Asia. Woody and nutty with a surprising scent of orange—comes into its own when toasted. Commonly paired with cumin in ground blends and pastes in South and Southeast Asia; also used whole as a pickling spice.

Cumin (*Cuminum cyminum*)
Native to the eastern Mediterranean but widespread since antiquity. Pungent, nutty, and warm with a hint of bitterness. Seeds resemble caraway and the best flavor emerges when toasted. Widely used in North Africa, the Middle East, South Asia, Mexico. It flavors oil in India, and ground cumin is added to meat, vegetable, and bean dishes; an important element of spice mixtures in many countries.

Ginger (*Zingiber officinale*)
Native to Southeast Asia; now widely grown, from Jamaica to Japan. A rhizome with many "fingers," ginger has a refreshing flavor with a hot kick. Used fresh, dried, or ground, in sweet and savory dishes. Fresh ginger is most esteemed for stir-fries, spice pastes, and as tea; ground ginger is popular in baking. "Stem ginger," preserved in syrup, is used for desserts.

Mustard (*Brassica juncea, B. nigra, B. hirta/Sinapsis alba*)
Native to Europe and Asia. The first species is brown, the second black, the third yellow. Round seeds are used whole as a pickling spice or fried in hot oil to flavor savory dishes in India. Mustard is best known as a pungently hot condiment with a nose-searing kick—the seeds are crushed to a paste or dried and powdered, then mixed with liquid.

Nutmeg (*Myristica fragrans*)
Native to Malaku, Indonesia. Nutmeg's botanical name provides a clue to why this spice has always been treasured throughout the world. Highly fragrant brown nut housed within an outer shell; best freshly grated. Used in desserts, baking, and in perfumed savory dishes of the Middle East and Asia; it is a perfect partner for spinach and cream.

Pepper (*Piper nigrum*)
Native to Southwest India. Black pepper is perhaps the most widely used spice in the world, valued as an aromatic hot seasoning. The small, round berries grow on vines: picked while still green, just before they ripen, they are often sold in brine or dried, occasionally sold fresh; when dried in the sun they turn black—the most familiar peppercorn; white peppercorns have had their outer skins removed. Pink peppercorns, often seen in mixed peppercorn packs, are from an unrelated plant, *Schinus terebinthifolius*.

Saffron (*Crocus sativus*)
Native to Persia and the Middle East. The most expensive spice in the world, because the stigmas of the saffron crocus have to be

hand-picked. Celebrated for its perfume, and for the golden color it brings to sweet and savory dishes. The bright red stigmas ("threads" or "strands") are usually infused in a little warm liquid before being added to a dish. Saffron's exquisite flavor graces rice dishes from Italy and Spain to the Middle East and South Asia; popular in desserts.

Sesame (*Sesamum indicum*)
Native to East Africa and South Asia. Small white, brown, or black seeds with a nutty flavor, emphasized by toasting. Appreciated for their texture in Japan and China; in the Middle East and eastern Mediterranean they are crushed to make tahini paste and sweet halva; the white variety is used throughout the world to coat snacks and bagels.

Turmeric (*Curcuma longa*)
Native to Southeast Asia. Brown rhizome with bright orange flesh; a member of the ginger family. Mostly available ground in the West, but also used fresh throughout Asia and the Middle East. Aromatic, peppery, and musky, it is used to spice oil and in curry pastes and powders. It is also a strong dye, giving a golden color to anything it touches.

Vanilla (*Vanilla planifolia*)
Native to Central America. The cured, long, dark brown beans are fragrant, with naturally occurring crystals of vanillin which provide scent and flavor. Good-quality vanilla is expensive. The bean may be used whole to flavor sauces or the poaching liquid for fruits; if split, the seeds can be scraped out and incorporated into desserts and ice cream. Also available as pure vanilla extract, or more concentrated essence. Synthetic vanilla flavoring is a common but very inferior product.

SECONDARY SPICES
Asafoetida (*Ferula asafoetida*)
Native to Persia and Afghanistan. Prized in Roman cooking, but now used pretty much only in western and southern India. A resin, mostly sold ground and sometimes in lumps, it is unpleasantly pungent in scent, but fabulous when cooked with other spices to flavor regional Indian dishes. It is often used by onion and garlic-eschewing Brahmins for its strong flavor. Available in Indian/Pakistani/Bangladeshi stores, and some supermarkets. Should be used in small doses.

Ajowan (*Carum ajowan*)
Native to Asia and Africa. Tiny seeds with a thyme-like flavor, used whole or ground, valued as a digestive and often partnered with gram flour in snacks like pakora. Available in Indian/Pakistani/Bangladeshi

stores, but if you can't find it you could substitute a little crushed dried thyme.

Amchoor (*Mangifera indica*)
The mango is native to India; amchoor is ground from dried unripe mangoes. It gives an excellent sour flavor; often part of chaat masala mixes used for snacks and salads. For sourness, you could also use *anardana* (below) or, in a pinch, lemon juice. Tamarind would be a better substitute. Available in Indian/Pakistani/Bangladeshi stores.

Black cumin (*Cuminum nigrum*)
Native to North India, Kashmir, Pakistan, Iran, and Afghanistan. Known as *kala jeera*; thin blackish seeds which are less bitter than regular cumin. Much valued in the above regions as a whole spice or as part of spice mixtures, such as Punjabi garam masala. Sold in Indian/Pakistani/Bangladeshi stores.

Brown cardamom (*Amomum subulatum*)
Native to India. Not a true cardamom, but a slightly larger brown pod with coarser flavor. Used in Kashmir, North India, and Pakistan as a whole spice and ground in some masalas. Sold in Indian/Pakistani/Bangladeshi stores.

Celery seed (*Apium graveolens dulce*)
Native to Europe. Brown seeds with strong celery flavor, usually found ground in celery salt and in some American spice blends.

Dill seed (*Anethum graveolens*)
Native to Europe. Small, flattish beige seeds with a lightly pungent flavor. Used as pickling spice, especially in Scandinavia and Russia, and to flavor bread, potatoes, and sometimes pastries; also used in breads in South Asia.

Fenugreek (*Trigonella foenum-graecum*)
Native to the eastern Mediterranean region. The yellowish seeds have a strong aroma, often encountered when opening ready-made curry powders. Hence people think of fenugreek as smelling of curry powder, but it is the other way around! Should be used in small quantities, especially if ground. Popular in Ethiopia, Yemen, and Afghanistan as well as South Asia. Available in South Asian, Ethiopian, and Middle Eastern stores.

Galangal (*Alpinia galanga*)
Native to Southeast Asia. A rhizome of the ginger family, generally known as "greater galangal," it has a ginger-like flavor and aroma, but tangier, with hints of lemongrass. Used fresh throughout Southeast Asia to flavor curries and soups. Available in Southeast Asian stores—as dried pieces, as a powder, and, if you're lucky, fresh.

Juniper berries (*Juniperus communis*)
Native to Europe and North America. Purple-black berries with a strong, aromatic, bitter-sweet flavor. Excellent with game, pork, and other meats, it appears in sausages, pâtés, terrines, marinades, sauces, and sauerkraut.

Mace (*see* Nutmeg)
The red, orange, or yellow tendril-like case which covers the outer shell of the nutmeg; although close in flavor and scent, mace is more refined and is highly desirable for all manner of sweet and savory dishes. For the best flavor, grind from the whole spice—sometimes called "blades." Available in Indian/Pakistani/Bangladeshi and Middle Eastern stores and gourmet stores.

Nigella (*Nigella sativa*)
Native to West Asia and southern Europe. The small black seeds are often mistakenly called onion seeds, although they have nothing to do with onions. Nigella has a most pleasant flavor when cooked, sharp but warm. Known as *kalonji* in India, where it is widely used to flavor vegetable and bean dishes, added to naan bread, or used in spice mixes. Nigella is also enjoyed in the Middle East and parts of Africa. Available in Indian/Pakistani/Bangladeshi stores and some African and Middle Eastern stores.

Poppy seed (*Papaver somniferum*)
Native to the Mediterranean region and Middle East. Tiny round white, brown, and black seeds used in breads and pastries, but further east in warming milk-based drinks or in sauces. Black seeds are most familiar in the West; white are common elsewhere.

Szechuan pepper/Fagara (*Zanthoxylum piperitum*)
Native to China. Brick-red berry with inner seeds from the prickly ash tree; best toasted before being used. Key component of Chinese five-spice mixture; also used in spiced salt seasoning. Has woody-peppery flavor, and a slight numbing effect. Sold in Chinese stores.

Star anise (*Illicium verum*)
Native to China and Vietnam. A beautiful, brown, star-shaped spice with a strong, perfumed anise scent and flavor. Ground, it permeates Chinese five-spice mixture; used whole—or broken into "petals"—it flavors soups, sauces, cooking liquids, and marinades. Available in Chinese stores.

Tamarind (*Tamarindus indica*)
Native to Africa and probably South Asia. Brown, lumpy, bean-like pod is usually sold in blocks, to be soaked in water, squeezed,

and strained to make tamarind water or concentrate. Adds delicious sour tang to savory dishes; popular in the Middle East and Asia. Makes a refreshing drink in parts of the Caribbean. Available in Southeast Asian, Indian/Pakistani/Bangladeshi and Middle Eastern stores. Also sold as ready-made concentrate.

Wasabi (Wasabia japonica)
Native to Japan; the root of the mountain hollyhock. Wasabi is often called Japanese horseradish because of the similar, very hot kick. Indispensable sushi condiment. Used freshly grated or as a paste in Japan; available in the West as a powder or ready-made paste, from Japanese and some Chinese stores, and in some supermarkets.

ELUSIVE SPICES

Anardana (Punica granatum)
The pomegranate is valued as a fruit and for its syrup in the Middle East and Asia. Dried ground pomegranate seeds, called anardana in India, are used for their sour flavor. Could substitute amchoor or tamarind. Available in Indian/Pakistani/Bangladeshi stores.

Annatto (Achiote/Achuete) (Bixa orellana)
Bright red seeds mainly used as a coloring agent—for example for cheese—but ground and used as a spice in Mexico and parts of South America. The taste is nutty and slightly tart. Available in Mexican and Filipino stores.

Assam gelugor (Garcinia atroviridis)
Very sour flavoring, used dried and sliced in Southeast Asia, especially in seafood dishes. Thai madan (G. schomburgkiana) has a similar sour taste, and is used fresh or dried in Thailand. Difficult to find outside Asia.

Chinese keys (Boesenbergia pandurata); Kencur (Kaempferia galanga); Lesser galangal (Alpinia officinarum); Zedoary (Curcuma zedoaria)
Lesser galangal is native to China; others are native to Southeast Asia. All are rhizomes from the ginger family; they have similar ginger/galangal-like flavors. Some are spicy, some fragrant, some bitter. Chinese keys (krachai) is the most individual in shape, and its lemon/ginger flavor is used in Thai cooking. Can be difficult to find outside Asia, except in some Chinese and Southeast Asian stores.

Cubeb (Piper cubeba)
Dark brown berries, like black peppercorns with a stalk or "tail." The flavor falls between allspice and black pepper, either of which could be substituted. Available in specialty stores and some mail order sources.

Grains of paradise/Melegueta pepper/Guinea pepper (Amomum melegueta)
Peppery brown seeds from West Africa. Important in medieval Europe, now confined to West and North Africa. Mail order sources.

Kokum (Garcinia indica)
Sticky black flavoring, derived from a tropical Asian fruit, with a tamarind-like sour taste. Used only in Western Indian cooking, especially in fish dishes; sometimes called fish tamarind. Some Indian stores stock it.

Long pepper (Piper longum)
Black, rattle-like pepper about 1/2 inch long, tasting very similar to black pepper, with a hint of warm sweetness. Highly valued by the ancient Greeks and Romans, but now rarely available in the West; try mail order sources.

Mahlab (Prunus mahaleb)
Oval, tan kernels of mahalab cherry. Dried and ground; used in Middle Eastern baking. Available in some Turkish and Middle Eastern stores or some mail order sources.

Nagkeshar/Cassia buds (See cassia)
Small, brown, dried unripe fruits of the cassia tree with their stalks; used whole in China for pickles and to flavor other dishes; used ground in some South Asian spice mixes. Difficult to find: sometimes available from South Asian stores; some mail order.

Salep/Sahlab (Orchis mascula)
Ground orchid root used as a thickener, but contributes its mild flavor to milky drinks in the Middle East; also be used in desserts. Difficult to find; try Middle Eastern stores.

Sansho (Zanthoxylum piperitum)
Close relative of Szechuan pepper, a berry from the Japanese prickly ash tree, dried and ground to a powder. Tangy flavor. Sprinkled over foods. Available from Japanese stores and mail order.

Sumac (Rhus coriaria)
Reddish-brown berries, dried and used as a souring agent throughout the Middle East. The ground spice is sprinkled over grilled meats and fish, and used in the Middle Eastern spice mixture zahtar. Available from Middle Eastern stores.

Triffla/Tirphal (Zanthoxylum rhetsa)
Black berry which only grows in Western India, with a woody, slightly bitter flavor; related to Szechuan pepper and sansho. Open berry with bitter seeds that are discarded; the berry is usually toasted before use. Difficult to find outside India.

mail order/ specialty stores

Spice Hunter
P.O. Box 8110
184 Surburban Rd
San Luis Obispo, CA 93403-8110
Tel: 800-444-3061
www.spicehunter.com

The Ethnic Grocer
www.ethnicgrocer.com
Tel: 866-438-4642

ASIAN
Pacific Rim Gourmet, i-Clipse, Inc.
11251 Coloma Road, Suite A
Gold River, CA 95670
Tel: 800-618-7575 / 916-852-7855
(outside continental U.S.)
Fax: 916-852-7911
www.pacificrim-gourmet.com

ThaiGrocer
1430 North Bosworth Avenue, Floor 1
Chicaco, IL 60622
Tel: 773-988-8424
Fax: 773-871-3969
www.thaigrocer.com

Katagiri (Japanese ingredients)
224 East 59th Street
New York, NY 10022
Tel: 212-755-3566
Fax: 212-752-4197
www.katagiri.com

Kam Man Food Products
200 Canal Street
New York, NY 10013
Tel: 212-571-0330

Gongshee (Chinese)
www.gongshee.com
Tel: 866-438-4642

Uwajimaya (East and Southeast Asian)
Tel: 206-624-3215
www.uwajimaya.com

AsiaFoods
www.asiafoods.com
Tel: 877-902-0841

Namaste (Indian)
www.namaste.com
Tel: 866-438-4642

AFRICAN
The South African Food Shop
Fullwood Plaza
11229 East Independence Blvd.,
Matthews, NC 28105
Tel: 704-849-2660 / 888-532-1433
www.southafricanfoodshop.com

MIDDLE EASTERN
Sultan's Delight
P.O. Box 90302
Brooklyn, NY 11209
Tel: 800-852-5046
Fax: 718-745-2563
www.sultansdelight.com

Kalustyan's
123 Lexington Avenue
New York, NY 10016
Tel: 212-685-3451
Fax: 212-683-8458
www.kalustyans.com

LATIN AMERICAN
Kitchen Market
218 Eighth Avenue
New York, NY 10011
Tel: 888-468-4433
www.kitchenmarket.com

www.mexgrocer.com
Tel: 877.463.9476

LOCAL INDIAN STORES

Apna Bazar
1275 Bloomfield Avenue
Fairfield, NJ 07004
Tel: 973-882-7990

Indian Groceries & Spices, Inc.'
8051 North Central Park
Skokie, IL 60071
Tel: 847-674-2480

ABC Groceries
10079 Sunset Strip
Sunrise, FL 33322
Tel: 954-746-7740

Little Market
3062 North Andrews Avenue
Ft. Lauderdale, FL 33311
Tel: 954-561-8606

Patel Brothers
37–27 74th Street
Jackson Heights, NY 11732
Tel: 718-898-3445

Bombay Bazar
1503 Finnigan's Lane
North Brunswick, NY 08902
Tel: 732-940-9148

bibliography

Thanks to the many books and authors who inspired
and enlightened me with historical knowledge:

K T Achaya, *Indian Food: A Historial Companion*,
Oxford University Press (Delhi), 1994; G Basan,
The Middle Eastern Kitchen, Kyle Cathie, 2001;
A L Basham, *The Wonder that was India*, Sidgwick
& Jackson, 1954; D J Boorstin, *The Discoverers*,
Penguin, 1986; J H Brierley, *Spices: The Story of
Indonesia's Spice Trade*, Oxford University Press
(Kuala Lumpur), 1994; C A Brock-Al Ansari, *The
Complete United Arab Emirates Cookbook*, 1994;
H Brown, *Studies in Venetian History (Vol I)*;
K C Chang (ed.), *Food in Chinese Culture*, Yale
University Press, 1977; C Corn, *The Scents of
Eden*, Kodansha America, 1998; E David, *Spices,
Salt and Aromatics in the English Kitchen*, Penguin,
1970; A Davidson, *The Oxford Companion to
Food*, Oxford University Press, 1999; D DeWitt,
The Chile Pepper Encyclopedia, Harper Collins,
1999; C Dille, S Belsinger, *Classic Southwest
Cooking*, Prima Publishing, 1993; M Dubey, B
Grewal (eds) *South India, Insight Guides*, 1992;
J L Flandrin, M Montanari (eds), *Food: A Culinary
History*, Penguin 2000; C Freeman, *Egypt, Greece,
and Rome*, Oxford University Press, 1996; R Hall,
Empires of the Monsoon, Harper Collins, 1996;
D T Hsiung, *The Chinese Kitchen*, Kyle Cathie,
2000; W Hutton, *Tropical Herbs and Spices*,
Periplus Editions, 1997; *J Keay, India: A History*,
Harper Collins, 2001; K F Kiple, K C Ornelas (eds),
Cambridge World History of Food (Vols I and II),
Cambridge University Press, 2000; O Logan, *Culture
and Society in Venice 1470–1790*, Batsford, 1972;
Colin Mackerras (ed.), *Eastern Asia: An Introductory
History*, Longman Cheshire, 1993; G Milton,
Nathaniel's Nutmeg, Hodder & Stoughton, 1999;
Jill Norman, *The Complete Book of Spices*,
Dorling Kindersley, 1990; Elizabeth Lambert Ortiz,
Complete Book of Caribbean Cooking, Ballantine
Books, 1986; J W Purseglove, E G Brown,
C L Green, S R J Robbins, *Spices (Vols I and II)*,
Longman, 1981; M Rodinson, A J Arberry, C Perry,
Medieval Arab Cookery, Prospect Books, 2001;
Helen Saberi, *Noshe Djan: Afghan Food and
Cookery*, Prospect Books, 1986; M Shaida, *The
Legendary Cuisine of Persia*, Penguin, 1994; A
Simmons, *The First American Cookbook*, Dover
Publications (facsimile of *American Cookery*, 1796),
1984; R Sokolov, *Why We Eat What We Eat*,
Summit Books, 1991; R Storey and D Mason,
Korea, Lonely Planet Publications, 1997; R Tannahill,
Food in History (rev. edn), Penguin, 1988; J Trager,
The Food Chronology, Henry Holt, 1995; A Wild,
The East India Company, Harper Collins, 2000.

index

conversion charts

Weights and measures have been rounded up
or down slightly to make measuring easier.

volume equivalents

american	metric	imperial
1 teaspoon	5 ml	
1 tablespoon	15 ml	
¼ cup	60 ml	2 fl.oz.
⅓ cup	75 ml	2½ fl.oz.
½ cup	125 ml	4 fl.oz.
⅔ cup	150 ml	5 fl.oz. (¼ pint)
¾ cup	175 ml	6 fl.oz.
1 cup	250 ml	8 fl.oz.

weight equivalents:

imperial	metric
1 oz.	25 g
2 oz.	50 g
3 oz.	75 g
4 oz.	125 g
5 oz.	150 g
6 oz.	175 g
7 oz.	200 g
8 oz. (½ lb.)	250 g
9 oz. 275 g	6 inches
10 oz.	300 g
11 oz.	325 g
12 oz.	375 g
13 oz.	400 g
14 oz.	425 g
15 oz.	475 g
16 oz. (1 lb.)	500 g
2 1b.	1 kg

measurements:

inches	cm
¼ inch	5 mm
½ inch	1 cm
¾ inch	1.5 cm
1 inch	2.5 cm
2 inches	5 cm
3 inches	7 cm
4 inches	10 cm
5 inches	12 cm
15 cm	
7 inches	18 cm
8 inches	20 cm
9 inches	23 cm
10 inches	25 cm
11 inches	28 cm
12 inches	30 cm

oven temperatures:

225°F	110°C	Gas ¼
250°F	120°C	Gas ½
275°F	140°C	Gas 1
300°F	150°C	Gas 2
325°F	160°C	Gas 3
350°F	180°C	Gas 4
375°F	190°C	Gas 5
400°F	200°C	Gas 6
425°F	220°C	Gas 7
450°F	230°C	Gas 8
475°F	240°C	Gas 9

picture credits

All photographs Peter Cassidy/© Ryland Peters & Small except:

Page 10 right, 11 left © Alastair Hendy **11 right** © Greg Elms/Lonely Planet Images **36 right** © Andy Tough **37** © FUNDACIÓN "C.R.D.O. AZAFRÁN DE LA MANCHA," Paseo de Castilla La Mancha, 15 – Bajo A, 45720 CAMUÑAS, (Toledo), ESPAÑA, Tel./Fax: 925/470284, e-mail: doam@doazafrandelamancha.com, http://www.doazafrandelamancha.com **56 right, 57** © Alastair Hendy **76 center and right, 77** © Alastair Hendy **100 right** © Keren Su/China Span/Lonely Planet Images **101 left** © Richard I'Anson/Lonely Planet Images **101 right** © Oliver Strewe/Lonely Planet Images **118 right** © Lee Foster/Lonely Planet Images **119 left** © Garrett Culhane/Lonely Planet Images **119 right** © Jerry Alexander/Lonely Planet Images.